THE ARCHITECTURE OF ENTERTAINMENT

THE
ARCHITECTURE OF
ENTERTAINMENT
LA IN THE TWENTIES

ROBERT WINTER
ALEXANDER VERTIKOFF

Gibbs Smith, Publisher
Salt Lake City

First Edition
10 09 08 07 06   5 4 3 2 1

Published by
Gibbs Smith, Publisher
P.O. Box 667
Layton, Utah 84041

1.800.748.5439 orders
www.gibbs-smith.com

Designed and produced by Deibra McQuiston
Jacket images by Alexander Vertikoff
Printed and bound in Hong Kong

Library of Congress Cataloging-in-Publication Data

Winter, Robert, 1924–
  The architecture of entertainment : L.A. in the twenties / Robert Winter ;
Alexander Vertikoff.— 1st ed.
      p. cm.
  Includes bibliographical references and index.
  ISBN 1-58685-797-5
  1. Architecture—California—Los Angeles—20th century.
  2. Eclecticism in architecture—California—Los Angeles.
  I. Vertikoff, Alexander. II. Title.

NA735.L55W56 2006
720.9794'9409042—dc22   2005027474

In memory of
David Gebhard and Harriet von Breton

Contents

ACKNOWLEDGMENTS

Many people have contributed to this book by giving advice and rounding up resources. Among these are Allene Archibald, Carrie Ballard, Gary Cowles, Linda Dishman, Bill Ellinger, Ron Fields, Jean France, Sid Gally, Patricia Gebhard, Ann Gray, Julie Heath, Diane Kanner, Pamela D. Kingsbury, Brenda Levin, Richard Longstreth, Ann Scheid Lund, Linda Harris Mehr, Merry Ovnick, Lian Partlow, Patricia Simpson, Leslie Steinberg, Nancy Wenzel, and Romy Wyllie.

Merry Ovnick read every sentence of this book. Her criticism has saved me from many embarrassments. Likewise, Ann Scheid Lund read the penultimate draft with special attention to the chapters on planning and gardens.

My neighbor Marcie Chan typed the manuscript and offered many welcome criticisms. Phil Freshman, who has edited another book for me, read this one with great care and understanding, as did Madge Baird and her staff at Gibbs Smith, Publisher: Linda Nimori, who deserves the highest praise for editing the manuscript and bringing the text and images together; Melissa Jordan, who did a superb job on the index; and Leticia Le Bleu, who spent endless hours organizing, scanning, and preparing the images for the designer and the printer. I am very grateful to Deibra McQuiston, who designed and produced this beautiful publication.

INTRODUCTION

W **E HAVE LONG BEEN FASCINATED** by interpretations of American life in the 1920s. The historian Frederick Lewis Allen considered the era rather silly. In his popular chronicle *Only Yesterday* (1931), he painted a picture of fun-filled times when flappers, booze, flagpole sitters, and jazz typified the spirit of release that at least some members of the post–World War I generation enjoyed. Other critics who assessed the period were gloomy. Malcolm Cowley wrote in his *Exile's Return* (1934) about young carefree Americans who escaped to Paris in the 1920s and then returned home just before daddy's money ran out in the Great Depression. He doubted that they learned very much during their self-indulgent odysseys. The literary critic Joseph Wood Krutch was even more dour about the decade in *The Modern Temper* (1929). He was among the many who condemned the period as a moral disaster.

This view of the early twentieth century was not new. In 1920 William Butler Yeats famously wrote in "The Second Coming" that "Things fall apart; the centre cannot hold." Even earlier, some late-nineteenth-century Amoses had prophesied, in the midst of an

expansive age, that something of major importance had gone wrong in modern life. The great British social critic William Morris (1834–1896) traced the problem to the dislocation that had occurred with rapid industrialization and the growth of cities. He would turn back the wheel of industry from the new consumer economy to the earlier producer economy, before the machine dominated people's lives. He and other idealists of the day envisioned returning to a simpler time, when hand labor presumably was pleasurable and people were not alienated from their work—and one another. In architecture the Morrisites signaled their displeasure with modern society by advocating styles that seemed to them appropriate for the handicraft tradition. In

Great Britain, this meant Gothic designs in public structures and the seventeenth-century country house in domestic architecture; in California, the Swiss chalet, the Japanese temple, and the Spanish mission epitomized the rejection of modern materialism.

After 1920, however, a different mindset prevailed. The idea of going backward in order to go forward had lost its charm. For example, Walter Gropius claimed to have based his ideas for revitalizing Weimar's school of arts and crafts, which he rechristened the Bauhaus after becoming its director in 1919, on Morris's principles; it would be a kind of cooperative that would revolutionize architecture and the other arts. But Gropius never accepted Morris's anti-modernism, believing that the goal of great craftsmanship could be accommodated to the conveyor belt and that beautiful things could be mass-produced. This approach and these methods would, Gropius thought, liberate architecture and the other arts from the dead hand of the past. His industrial esthetic appealed to people disillusioned by World War I and by the Victorian ideas that had helped pave the way to war. Adopting it, they believed, would be a way to start over.

There was also another, somewhat frivolous, approach to the problem of disillusionment. Why not fantasize and use historic architectural styles as adventurous escapades? Styles would not be chosen, as they

■ PAGE 11: Flappers spend time at an Art Deco miniature golf course.
FACING: Mission Inn (1902), Riverside; Arthur B. Benton, architect. It was
designed to symbolize a retreat from the city and its busy-ness. ABOVE: The
Bauhaus (1925–26), Dessau, Germany; Walter Gropius, architect. This
school was the center of the early Modern movement.

■ LEFT: Sphinx Realty advertisement: architecture sculpture by Lee Lawrie, used as advertising. RIGHT: Batchelder advertisement: advertising sells tiles with the help of a flapper and a peacock. FACING: Batchelder House (1909), a Craftsman bungalow, Pasadena; Ernest A. Batchelder, architect.

were by the Arts and Crafts devotees, for their reference to idealized golden ages in the past but rather for their ability to create drama in lives jaded by the dreary materialism of the Machine Age. The burgeoning travel industry of the 1920s was one impetus for this new ahistorical treatment of architectural styles. The number of Americans traveling at home and abroad increased dramatically during that decade with such enterprises as the University of Travel that organized trips, mainly to Europe, for schoolteachers and other middle-class people on vacation and for young adults whose parents had the means to broaden their minds. A few weeks in Europe exposed these American travelers to great monuments of art and architecture. The depth of this tourist experience might be questioned but not the pleasure it afforded.

This was also a period when advertising was becoming more subtle and sophisticated. As Richard Longstreth noted in his book *City Center to Regional Mall* (1997), "Architecture was increasingly seen as a contributor to effective merchandising." Consider the titles of a few contemporary articles on the subject: "Shop Fronts Must Advertise" (*Building Age*, January 1930), "Is Good Architectural Design a Paying Investment?" (*Pacific Coast Architect*, March 1924), "Architecture for the Merchant" (*Architect and Engineer*, June 1929), and "The Spanish Stores of Morgan, Walls and Clements" (*Architectural Forum*, June 1929). Some critics dismissed buildings created in the first two decades of the century as boring, claiming their architects were too sparing of ornamental detail. The historic styles could be used to give color to the urban scene.

A telling example of the cozy relationship between advertising and architecture in the 1920s was the promotion of bungalows. The idea of the one-story or story-and-a-

"Just a little different" Bungalows

Edw. E. Sweet Designing and Building Co.
Los Angeles, Cal.

■ *Sweet's Bungalow Book:* a typical bungalow designed by Alfred Heineman. Sweet's was only one of the many companies that spread the bungalow craze by mail. They warned the reader to avoid simply turning the few drawings over to a carpenter. Sweet's would provide complete plans for $10 to $15.

half house for people of moderate means literally sold itself when its advantages were publicized. Sears, Roebuck and other mail-order houses even produced and touted prefabricated bungalows that could be transported anywhere in the country. The Pacific Ready-cut Company, based in Los Angeles, advertised that buyers of its small houses could choose among various styles, all approved by architectural experts.

By far the greatest promoters of appealing and imaginative—albeit esthetically superficial—architectural styles were the moviemakers. By 1929 an estimated twenty to thirty million Americans were watching movies every week, and the film industry was claiming the largest portion of the average American's recreation budget. As Lary May noted in his *Screening Out the Past* (1980), the movies' depictions of glamorous surroundings and foreign cultures encouraged "a quest for a more exotic life." They were a means of escape, as were the period revivals in architecture that they often displayed. Merry Ovnick, a historian at California State University, Northridge, suggests that because most films made in the 1920s were silent, directors and designers created dramatic atmosphere by featuring precipitous rooflines and deep architectural indentations; this was the architectural equivalent of silent-screen actors using exaggerated facial expressions to convey emotion. The use of styles in the movies caused their audiences to expect more drama in their architecture.

It may be argued, then, that movies prompted a great many Americans to realize for the first time that architecture was, like other arts, a vehicle of expression. As the architectural historian Dietrich Neumann wrote in an article titled "Before and After Metropolis" in his *Film Architecture* (1999), "Architecture had begun to act in movies; skyscrapers had risen to the status of movie stars." D. W. Griffith's Babylonian set for *Intolerance* (1916) and Cecil B. DeMille's sets for *The King of Kings* (1927) nicely illustrate Neumann's point. These and other filmed extravaganzas introduced Americans to grandiose interpretations of ancient architecture—and they loved it.

That the movie people knew what they were doing is evident in an article DeMille wrote in 1925, "Motion Pictures and Architecture," for the *Bulletin* of the Allied Architects of Los Angeles. "As the most pervasive influence life has yet known," he asserted, in the overblown but canny rhetoric of his profession, "motion pictures have had a definite influence on trends taken by architecture within the last decade." He believed that movies attacked the insularity of Americans by giving them the world—life, customs, buildings—in just a few hours.

Undoubtedly, the masses were becoming increasingly aware of architecture. But as it was democratized, was it also being trivialized? Many critics thought so. Lewis

■ ABOVE: Movie set—D. W. Griffith's *Intolerance* (1916–19). This set was so popular that it was exhibited at the intersection of Hollywood and Sunset boulevards for several years after it was filmed. FACING: Movie set—Cecil B. DeMille's *King of Kings* (1927). Obviously this set pictures debauchery at its worst. Note the expressions on the faces of the actors in the foreground.

Mumford, a committed advocate of William Morris's principles and one of the century's most respected critics of architectural trends, deplored what he called "the architecture of escape." He lamented in the *New Republic*, August 12, 1925, that

> *Whenever we can break loose from our anonymous cubicles, our standardized offices, our undifferentiated streets, we abandon ourselves to pure romance. . . . Who has not been tempted to turn off the radiator, so he might warm his hands at an open fire. Who has not tried to fancy what life might be if he could tarry a while in Chipping Camden [sic] or Bybury? . . . The critical weakness of the romantic architect is that he is employed in creating an environment into which people may escape from a sordid workaday world, whereas the real problem of architecture is to remake the workaday world so that people will not wish to escape it.*

As late as the 1940s, others were still denigrating early-twentieth-century "escape" architecture. One was the educator and historic-preservation advocate James Marston Fitch in his *American Building* (1948):

> *At first glance, the period from 1900 to 1933 appears to be an esthetic wasteland; and a closer scrutiny of the individual buildings of the period does little to correct that first impression. Those*

> *structures which were hailed as the landmarks of the time—the Woolworth Tower, the San Francisco Exposition, the Mizner story-book houses in Florida, the Chicago Tribune's Gothic extravaganza, the Triangle in Washington: they all leave today's critic unimpressed. These buildings are so colorless and without significance, so magnificently sterile, as to leave one non-plussed.*

Today such sentiments seem strange—Chicago's Tribune Tower (1925) "colorless" and "manifestly sterile"? The eclectic buildings created in the 1920s may sometimes be bizarre and even laughable, but they also can be delightful and often provocative.

Santa Catalina Island, only a few miles off the shore of Wilmington and a part of Los Angeles County, has been a resort community since the late nineteenth century. Its widespread fame came after 1919, however, when William Wrigley Jr., the Chicago chewing-gum tycoon, bought the island from the Banning family and began its development on a very large scale. He opened a galena mine, a rock quarry, and even a plant that produced decorative tiles, which he called Catalina Clay Products. In love with the island, he built a house on a hill that overlooked the harbor and village of Avalon. From his study, he could watch his Chicago Cubs work out during their winter training in an area directly below the house.

Wrigley was a natural promoter. He planned a tourist industry that would bring thousands of travelers to the island. In fact,

based only on steamer counts, 622,000 tourists visited Avalon in 1926, and 700,000 in 1930. They came to see nature in the raw on their visits to the interior of the island, and were fascinated by marine life in the clear waters of the bay, which they viewed from glass-bottom boats. Although mildly interested in the ecology of the island, Wrigley all but destroyed the picturesque shoreline of the bay by leveling its surrounding rocky outcroppings (one was called Sugarloaf) in order and appearance to build the Casino. His son had seen a pleasure palace that had a ballroom over a theater, and he convinced his father that a similar structure would enhance the scenery. In 1928 Wrigley hired architects Walter Webber and Sumner Spaulding to contrive a fantasy that would be "a place of entertainment," melding Islamic and Spanish Revival motifs, and John Gabriel Beckman to design murals for the entrance porch and the interior theater and ballroom. With its mighty Page pipe organ, which included bird whistle and automobile horn stops, the building was complete and has been a success even to the present day.

In an article for *New Mexico Studies in the Fine Arts* (1982), David Van Zanten, an architectural historian at Northwestern University, defended in particular the neo-Gothic tendencies of the architects of the 1920s. Take, for example, the Tribune Tower (1922–25) in Chicago. The design of the exterior of its last stage was clearly modeled on the spire of the "Tour de Buerre" attached to the medieval cathedral at Rouen. But instead of performing a functional role as they had in supporting the ancient structure, the flying buttresses on the Tribune Tower were hung from the steel frame. Van Zanten argues that its architects, Raymond Hood and John Mead Howells, were aiming at a picturesque effect that was just as valid as an expression of function. He saw the tower as "an architecture of entertainment . . . significant in its own time as a witty background to brighten up the new industrial cities." After all, he added, during the 1920s "mere entertainment was the stated objective of Satie, Ravel and Poulenc, composers whom we now celebrate. . . . A good piece of entertainment has many of the features of art: it is convincing, it is well paced, it is absorbing, thrilling and witty. . . . The only thing that entertainment lacks is purpose. . . ." Van Zanten is of course talking about the exterior of ornamented buildings that may be perfectly adapted to their intended function on their interiors but be completely fanciful in the way they face the public. Needless to say, that describes a great deal of what we see in the architecture of the twenties.

■ LEFT: Rouen Cathedral (begun A.D. 1200), Rouen, Normandy, France. The famous "Butter Tower" (1485–1507) miraculously escaped destruction during World War II. RIGHT: Chicago Tribune Tower (1925), Chicago; Hood and Howells, architects. The Tribune Tower owes a great deal to its ancestor—the Rouen Cathedral.

THE CASINO AT AVALON
SANTA CATALINA ISLAND

WALTER WEBBER, ARCHITECT
SUMNER SPAULDING, ARCHITECT

 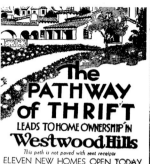 

THE FACE OF THE CITY

THE CLICHÉD OBSERVATION THAT LOS ANGELES is a collection of suburbs in search of a city—the number of suburbs varies—supports urban historian Robert M. Fogelson's contention that it is "a fragmented metropolis." For many years the various communities throughout Los Angeles County remained independent of one another; Pasadena, Santa Monica, and Long Beach, for example, have never been incorporated into the City of Los Angeles. Yet in spite of obvious differences in character, these many disparate communities have long had much in common. All of them were linked (and some were created) by railroads and streetcar lines; the automobile strengthened these ties. Their residents pursued similar goals—to attain health and wealth; they saw the freedom to do so as a fact of life.

Another characteristic shared by these separate entities and the metropolis as a whole is that they still boast many examples of architecture dating back to the 1920s. Several factors converged to make the 1920s an extremely active period in Los Angeles architecture. One of the most significant was a population explosion that began with the coming

of the transcontinental railroad in the late 1870s and the economic boom of the 1880s. By 1910 Los Angeles County had about half a million inhabitants; twenty years later, approximately 2.2 million people lived in the greater Los Angeles area, many of them lured by the climate, movies, or oil.

Before the Southern Pacific Railroad laid tracks from San Francisco to Los Angeles in 1876, thereby giving Southern California a transcontinental link, a number of local rail lines were already operating. The first, completed in 1869, connected the central city to the new harbor in San Pedro to the south. Soon four other lines—to San Fernando, San Bernardino, Anaheim, and Santa Monica—formed a network that made it easy to travel to and from previously isolated communities in Los Angeles County.

Henry E. Huntington began consolidating these short lines in 1901 when he formed the Pacific Electric Railway; it became one of the finest urban transportation systems in the nation. In its heyday, Pacific Electric's fifty-foot-long "Big Red Cars" moved at a clip of forty to fifty miles per hour over more than a thousand miles of track that reached from the San Fernando Valley to the foothills of the San Gabriel Mountains, down the coast from Santa Monica to Balboa Island, and inland to San Bernardino and Redlands. The popularity of the Red Cars waned with the proliferation of the automobile, and by

1962 they were extinct. Yet while they lasted, they were instrumental in developing the urban pattern of the region, as the late historian Reyner Banham recognized in his *Los Angeles: The Architecture of Four Ecologies* (1971).

Because the interurban cars made travel over a vast area simple and affordable, they encouraged low-density growth. In 1930 more than 50 percent of the land in the Los Angeles basin was still undeveloped. Because the single-family dwelling was the rule, an aerial view taken around that time would have revealed a cityscape almost devoid of tall structures. Although some multistory apartment houses had begun appearing early in the century, Los Angeles was a horizontal city for many decades. Not until 1957 could buildings legally exceed a height limit of one hundred and fifty feet.

Because the population was spread out over a large landmass, lots were among the cheapest in the country. They also were relatively large: frontages of forty to fifty feet and depths of one hundred fifty feet were common. The bungalow was especially popular because its one- or one-and-a-half-story design provided ample room indoors and enough space outdoors for yards and gardens. These dwellings thus afforded their owners a sense of country living. In *City Center to Regional Mall* (1997), Richard Longstreth describes the appeal of these residential areas:

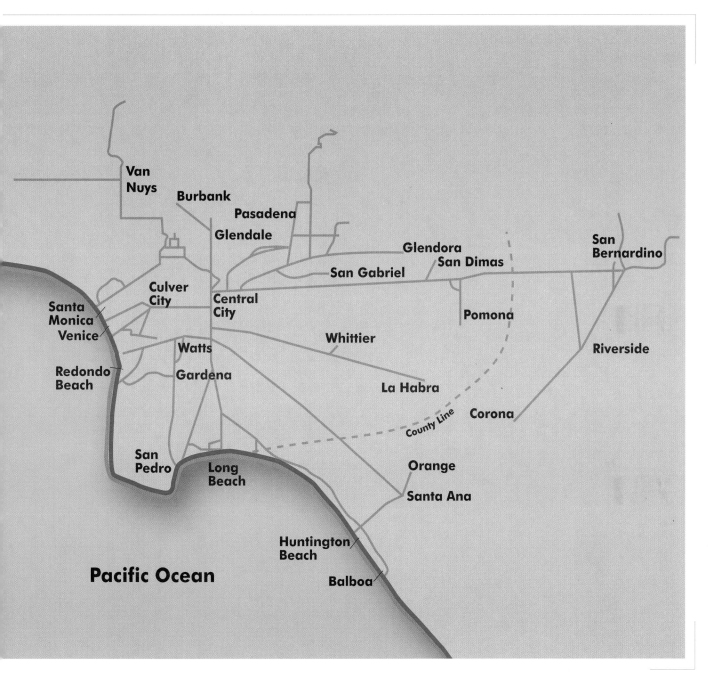

Van Nuys

Burbank

Pasadena

Glendale

Glendora

San Dimas

San Gabriel

San Bernardino

Culver City

Central City

Pomona

Santa Monica

Venice

Whittier

Riverside

Redondo Beach

Watts

Gardena

La Habra

County Line

Corona

San Pedro

Long Beach

Orange

Santa Ana

Pacific Ocean

Huntington Beach

Balboa

■ PAGE 29: Aladdin Bungalow—"The Pasadena": Sunroom entrance from the living room. See also the photo essay for the Aladdin Bungalow in "Housing for the Masses" on page 86. ABOVE: Route of the Pacific Electric Railway, 1923. Based on the map in Reyner Banham's book *Los Angeles: The Architecture of Four Ecologies* (1971), page 80, which he redrew from an illustration in an old Red Car book.

In [Los Angeles] communities such as South Gate, Maywood, Belvedere, and Montebello, the freestanding house set in a verdant yard along a quiet street, rather than the tenement or flat, became the standard. Realtors promoted the difference [from other large American cities] strenuously and sometimes with élan. . . . Yet the idyllic image advertised often did not stray far from the actuality. A significant portion of the skilled blue-collar populace could live much like their white-collar counterparts—more modestly but otherwise in the same mode, partaking of a spacious environment, tied to municipal services, often agreeably removed from the workplace, commuting by streetcar or by automobile.

By the 1920s several transportation arteries connected the central business and theater district of Los Angeles to the suburbs. Boyle Heights was the first such community served by streetcars and then by the Red Cars (and Yellow Cars). In another direction, Wilshire Boulevard cut its way west from the heart of downtown through Westlake Park (now MacArthur Park) and began picking up communities on its meandering route to Santa Monica and the ocean. An upscale branch of Bullocks Department Store, resplendent with Art Deco touches, murals, and sculpture, arose on Wilshire just west of Westlake Park in 1929. Farther west on the boulevard, between La Brea and Fairfax avenues, realtor A. W. Ross had

begun developing a commercial strip in 1924 after the repeal of a zoning ordinance limiting that area to residences. By decade's end, the strip was known as Miracle Mile, and it became home to dozens of upscale retail shops whose appeal was aimed mainly at people in their cars.

By the end of the 1920s, central Los Angeles also had commercial competitors. Hollywood, founded in the late 1880s by Methodist temperance advocates who proscribed both liquor and early picture shows in the city, became the capital of American moviemaking. Theaters, restaurants, banks, and other commercial structures were built along the boulevard bearing its name. Much of Hollywood's flamboyant architecture from this period still stands.

Still farther out on Wilshire Boulevard, the Janss Investment Company was developing Westwood Village, a Spanish Revival–style commercial district and adjacent residential area; by 1929 the heights north of the village had become the Romanesque campus of the University of California, Los Angeles (UCLA). Far to the south Long Beach was attracting thousands of people, many from Iowa but also

■ FACING: Bullocks Wilshire Department Store (1929), Los Angeles; John and Donald Parkinson, architects. Bullocks was the venture that encouraged the Wilshire commercial strip to continue westward to Santa Monica and the ocean. See also the photo essay for Bullocks Wilshire in "Modernism" on page 144.

■ Grauman's Chinese Theater (1927),
now Mann's, Hollywood; Meyer and
Holler, architects. China, somewhat
misconstrued.

from other states. Soon it was filled with new commercial buildings and acre upon acre of bungalows. It was linked with central Los Angeles by a corridor of city property that cut through unincorporated land all the way to neighboring San Pedro, the port of Los Angeles. Even though an earthquake in March 1933 demolished a great deal of the Long Beach business district, and a mindless effort at urban renewal in the 1960s and 1970s wiped out much of the remaining old construction, it still preserves some important structures dating from the 1920s.

Pasadena, to the northeast, is another city in Los Angeles County that recalls the 1920s. Its magnificent Beaux-Arts Civic Center, as well as its classic bungalows and lavish mansions, reflect the city's glory days. Glendale also has its share of architecture reflective of the decade. In fact, since every inhabited area in the county experienced a boom in the 1920s, even then-small communities such as Monrovia and Claremont in the San Gabriel Valley and Van Nuys in the San Fernando Valley benefited from the development of the distinctive period styles of the 1920s.

During the urban-renewal craze of the 1950s and 1960s, many of San Francisco's

handsome buildings from the 1920s and earlier were torn down and replaced with high-rise structures of questionable merit. Fortunately, however, several Victorian-era residential districts (most notably Haight-Ashbury) remained intact, having also survived the April 1906 earthquake and fire. Ironically, exactly the opposite phenomenon occurred in downtown Los Angeles after World War II. There, hundreds of Beaux-Arts commercial buildings, many from the 1920s, were spared when developers and city planners replaced the old Victorian residential district that rose directly above the main downtown streets, with tall buildings of mediocre modernism. Since Los Angeles did not take off economically until the close of the nineteenth century, the destruction of Victorian houses on Bunker Hill erased most of the downtown's early domestic architecture. Yet even today the business district boasts a remarkable collection of buildings dating from about 1900 to 1930.

By 1918 sixteen medium-rise office and commercial buildings had been erected in downtown Los Angeles; there were 72 by 1925 and 103 in 1929. Together they comprised the most extensive business core of any American city of comparable size. The physical appearance of these buildings depended mainly upon when they were constructed—either before or after World War I. The earlier buildings exemplified the Beaux-Arts principle of exterior organization: essentially a classical column, base, shaft, and capital, with detail added. Many contemporary critics complained that these Beaux-Arts buildings were dull and needed more ornament.

The Los Angeles buildings of the 1920s were anything but dull! Covered with exterior detail and often with color, they reflected every imaginable style. Theater facades ranged from French baroque to Mayan. Gothic detail might adorn a building next door to one decked out in Spanish Churrigueresque. Art Deco, almost as popular in Los Angeles as in New York, figured prominently in this mélange. This was clearly architecture as entertainment—superficial, to be sure, but also diverting and often appealing.

■ FACING: Eastern Columbia Building (1929), Los Angeles; Claude Beelman, architect. The new and the old: the fanciful Eastern Columbia building is set off next to an older, much more subdued building of the second decade of the twentieth century.

PLANNING THE
"CITY BEAUTIFUL"

SINCE THE BEGINNING OF AMERICA'S HISTORY, planning has determined the design of its cities. In the seventeenth century, Spanish settlers imposed Roman order on new villages centered around plazas in the Southwest, just as the Puritans adapted the organization of the English manor to the townships of New England. In the eighteenth century, James Oglethorpe and William Penn proposed plans for Savannah and Philadelphia, and Pierre-Charles L'Enfant based his plan for Washington, D.C., on the design of Versailles.

Urban planners in the American West of the late nineteenth century faced a unique problem. The gridiron plan first imposed on territories included in the Northwest Ordinance (1787) was applied to the new towns of the pioneers, probably due to the influence of the Freemasons, who were severe geometers. While this rigid north-south, east-west grid made for orderly development, it also produced many visually dull settlements. Exceptions were cities such as San Francisco; because they were situated on hills, the straight lines of the grids provided picturesque excitement when imposed upon the rough terrain.

Considering the ugliness of most American cities in the late nineteenth century, it is no wonder that the World's Columbian Exposition, set in Chicago in 1893, created a sensation. Daniel H. Burnham (1846–1912), a successful Chicago architect, and Frederick Law Olmsted (1822–1903), already famous as the landscape architect of Central Park in New York City, developed the exposition site. The result was a complex of broad avenues, well-meaning sculpture, lagoons, vistas, and white-plaster buildings designed by some of the country's most prestigious architects. This "Great White City" attracted thousands of visitors and nationwide publicity. It also inspired planning commissions in the era of Progressivism to consider esthetic transformations of their own cities. Burnham himself led the way and in 1909 proposed an elaborate "City Beautiful" plan for Chicago: wide avenues would cut diagonally through the original gridiron and make the most of both the Chicago River and the Lake Michigan shoreline. Burnham traveled across the United States, proposing similar ideas for other American cities. Unfortunately, none of these plans was fully implemented, but many civic centers were proposed and eventually built, albeit on a smaller scale than Burnham envisioned.

In Los Angeles there was talk as early as 1900 of creating a City Beautiful civic center. The private City Planning Association, formed in 1913, pressured the city fathers to commission a plan. In 1917 landscape architect and engineer J. S. Rankin presented a comprehensive proposal whose sole lasting accomplishment was its recommendation of a site for the civic center. The only significant buildings that resulted from the continuing discussion and the jostling of several ambitious schemes were the Hall of Justice (1925) and City Hall (1926–28), both designed by a consortium of major architectural offices (those of John C. Austin, John and Donald Parkinson, and Albert C. Martin) that called itself the Allied Architects of Los Angeles.

Today the fourteen-story, gray-granite Beaux-Arts Hall of Justice has been virtually abandoned because of seismic problems. But the twenty-eight-story City Hall, having been restored from basement to tower—including its decoration, artwork, and furnishings—is in excellent shape. Both inside and out, it reveals the obvious influence of the state capitol building (1919–32) in Lincoln, Nebraska, designed by Bertram G. Goodhue (1869–1924). The general massing and arrangement of windows are the same, although the design of the tower cap (evidently based on a conjectural model of the ancient Mausoleum at Halicarnassus) is an imaginative touch; it encloses a lofty room

with a frieze bearing flamboyant declarations of civic pride, created by Nebraska philosopher and poet Hartley Burr Alexander, who had done similar work on Goodhue's Nebraska State Capitol.

Another Goodhue associate, Austin Whittlesey, designed the entrance rotunda, the mayor's office, and the council chamber. As in the Nebraska capitol, these interiors combine Byzantine and Islamic effects and

basilica-like space. It is all very grand. Suitable for a city on the make, it seemed perfectly fitting that motion-picture-palace impresario Sid Grauman was chosen to direct the building's three-day-long dedication festivities held in April 1928.

According to the master plan that had been adopted in 1927 after prolonged wrangling and compromise, several more city and county buildings were to be constructed in the near future. But the Depression intervened. A return to the City Beautiful civic-center concept was postponed until after World War II, when several government edifices, such as the Hall of Administration Building (1956–61) and the Los Angeles County Courthouse (1958), were erected— all of them dull. Two decades after the war, a trio of theater buildings, collectively called the Music Center (1964–67), arose, as did a new Department of Water and Power Building (1963–64). Considering the city's dependence upon both the entertainment industry and an adequate water supply, it seems appropriate that these structures figure so prominently in the Los Angeles Civic Center.

In nearby Pasadena a more successful Beaux-Arts plan was developed in the 1920s. The late David Gebhard, an architectural historian at the University of California, Santa Barbara, once said that there was only one finer civic-center plan than that of Pasadena—Sir Edwin Lutyen's 1913 design for New Delhi, India. The instigator of Pasadena's comprehensive plan was George Ellery Hale, an astronomer who was sent to the city by the Carnegie Foundation in 1903 to construct and administer an observatory— as it turned out, the last building Daniel Burnham would design—on Mount Wilson. A native of Chicago, Hale drew upon his memory of the 1893 World's Columbian Exposition to create a City Beautiful civic center in his adopted hometown.

In 1923, with other members of the city planning commission, including tile-maker Ernest Batchelder, Hale established a com-mittee to select the architects for buildings on a Beaux-Arts plan that had been developed by the Chicago firm of Bennett, Parsons, Frost and Thomas, which had inherited the mantle of Burnham. The firm had composed a cross-axial plan with a city hall at its center and a civic auditorium and a public library at either end of a north-south minor axis running along what is today Garfield Avenue. Double rows of trees would line the major axis leading west from city hall along Holly Street, between the already existing YWCA (1920–22; Julia Morgan) and the YMCA (1912, A. B. Benton; remodeled 1926, Marston, Van Pelt, and Maybury).

Ignoring Hale's reservations, the jury agreed to commission only California architects for the main buildings. The prominent San Francisco firm of John Bakewell Jr. and Arthur Brown Jr., which designed that city's magnificent city hall after the earthquake and fire of April 1906, was chosen to create a comparable but smaller version in Pasadena. After several false starts at doing a facade that would evoke the *campanario* (bell tower) at the San Gabriel Mission on a grand scale, they instead blended elements from the Escorial near Madrid with the dome of the Invalides in Paris and the New Cathedral in Salamanca. The result, built between 1925 and 1927, was (and is) great theater.

Less dramatic but equally eclectic is the Pasadena Civic Auditorium (1932), designed

by the Pasadena architectural firm of Cyril Bennett and Fitch Haskell, who chose a mainly Italian Renaissance palazzo form that is complemented on the interior with a medley of Pompeiian decorative images.

Another local architect, Myron Hunt (1868–1952), designed the Pasadena Public Library (1927). The street side of the building exhibits Hunt's usual rather-dry interpretation of the Spanish Renaissance, relieved by a dashing Plateresque (silversmith-like) entrance as a centerpiece. As jury member Ernest Batchelder correctly predicted, "The library is a building that we will love the more the longer we live with it."

■ FACING: City Hall (1927), Pasadena; John Bakewell Jr. and Arthur Brown Jr., architects. The City Hall is a glorious example of elaborate stage scenery. ABOVE: Civic Auditorium (1932), Pasadena; Bennett and Haskell, architects. This building is the anchor of the south end of the Beaux-Arts minor axis.

Long Beach also attempted to implement City Beautiful ideas in the 1920s, but the Civic Auditorium (1930–32), designed by New York City architects J. Harold MacDowell and W. Horace Austin of Long Beach, and located at the south end of an axis along Long Beach Boulevard, was about the only result. There were, however, some interesting local attempts at Beaux-Arts planning in the design of college and university campuses during this period. Occidental College, founded in Boyle Heights in 1887,

moved to Highland Park in the 1890s. To distance itself from the Santa Fe Railroad tracks, it moved again—to Eagle Rock in 1914. The architects picked to design the new campus were Myron Hunt and Elmer Grey (1871–1963), who already had done exemplary work in the Los Angeles area. Their partnership dissolved in 1910, just as they were beginning to design the campus; as a result, Hunt was the sole planner.

Hunt was another former Chicagoan familiar with Daniel Burnham's ideas as they had been realized at the 1893 Chicago fair, and then further articulated in 1909 as his citywide Chicago Plan. The Beaux-Arts-inspired master plan Hunt completed for Occidental College in 1913 initially called for the construction of three buildings, which opened for occupancy in 1914. In collaboration with H. C. Chambers, Hunt designed ten more buildings on the Occidental campus during the 1920s and, in spite of the Great Depression, an additional seven in the 1930s. To accommodate certain new requirements, he somewhat revised the original plan in the 1920s but the basic cross-axial design remained. In a letter to Remsen Bird, the president of Occidental in the 1920s and '30s, he quoted Daniel Burnham's famous maxim, "Make no little plans."

■ Facing: Public Library (1927), Pasadena; Myron Hunt and H. C. Chambers, architects. The elaborate entrance is somewhat uncharacteristic of Hunt, whose buildings are usually bland. BELOW: Johnson Student Center (1928), formerly Freeman Union, Occidental College, Eagle Rock; Myron Hunt and H. C. Chambers, architects. A Spanish Revival building of the 1920s.

FACING: Public Library (1926), front facade, Los Angeles; Bertram G. Goodhue and Carleton M. Winslow, architects.

LEFT: Public Library. tower detail, south side.

BELOW: American Legion Headquarters Building (1929), Hollywood; Weston and Weston (Eugene Weston Jr.), architect. The Westons were friends of Bertram Goodhue.

GOODHUE & GOODHUESQUE

IN THE TWENTIES

"THE CITY CAME INTO BEING TO PRESERVE LIFE, IT EXISTS FOR THE GOOD LIFE"

ABOVE: Los Angeles City Hall, Tower Room (1926–28), Los Angeles; Allied Architects: John C. Austin, John and Donald Parkinson, and Albert C. Martin (see also pages 41 and 43). The poetic inscriptions near the ceiling were created by Hartley Burr Alexander, who also fashioned those in the Nebraska State Capitol.

ABOVE: Wilshire Ward Chapel (1928), The Church of Jesus Christ of Latter-day Saints (Mormon), Los Angeles; Harold W. Burton, architect.
FACING ABOVE: Wilshire Ward Chapel, exterior detail showing the marks of the forms into which the concrete was poured.

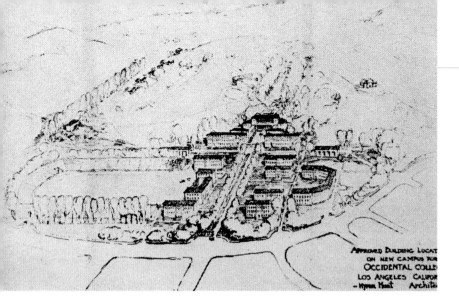

■ Design for Occidental College (1913), Pasadena; Myron Hunt, architect. Though major changes have been made to this plan through the years, the basic elements have been adhered to. Hunt was influenced by Burnham's layout of the Chicago World's Fair as well as by Thomas Jefferson's plan for the University of Virginia.

Hunt devised his Occidental College plan around the time that he and Grey also were designing the new campus of the Throop Polytechnic Institute in Pasadena. George Ellery Hale, who was a member of the Throop's board of trustees in addition to his other public roles, liked Hunt and Grey's Beaux-Arts design, but when he saw the 1915 plan that Bertram G. Goodhue, by this time a famous American architect, had made for the Panama-California Exposition in San Diego, he realized Goodhue's greater mastery. The Throop trustees were equally impressed. In the same year, they approved Hunt and Grey's plan with ideas from the Goodhue office. This was just four years before Throop, a trade school with a liberal-arts accent, metamorphosed

into the California Institute of Technology (Caltech)—modeled on Hale's alma mater, the Massachusetts Institute of Technology (MIT). Goodhue, who claimed to hate the École des Beaux-Arts, nevertheless expanded and elaborated upon Hunt and Grey's cross-axial design. Had his plan been fully carried out, it would have competed for excellence with the Pasadena Civic Center, in which Hale was also involved.

During the 1920s the Los Angeles architectural firm of John and Donald Parkinson was drawing upon similar ideas at the University of Southern California (USC). Its cross-town rival, the University of California at Los Angeles (UCLA), commissioned a Beaux-Arts master plan from George W. Kelham, a San Francisco architect who incorporated a grand staircase at the north end of its major axis—a Beaux-Arts dream—connecting the upper campus to the lower one. Just to the south was Westwood Village, which the Janss Investment Company had planned as a quaint, primarily Mediterranean-style commercial and residential area to complement the university's Romanesque imagery.

Two other local variations on the City Beautiful theme deserve mention—Beverly Hills and Palos Verdes Estates, both designed by landscape architects and both directly related to the ideas of Frederick Law Olmsted. Wilbur Cook, a New York City landscape architect who had worked for Olmsted, developed the master plan for Beverly Hills. He clearly had in mind Olmsted and Burnham's plan for the 1893 World's Columbian Exposition when the Rodeo Land and Water Company, led by real estate developer Burton E. Green, asked him in 1906 to design a city for upper-class residents. In line with Olmsted and Burnham's Beaux-Arts concern to render a plan according to proposed functions, Cook (working with Myron Hunt) separated the commercial from the residential district; he cleverly skewed a portion of the commercial area so that its streets were perpendicular to Santa Monica Boulevard, which runs diagonally from northeast to southwest. Above the boulevard, he continued the streets of the commercial gridiron into a proposed residential district but laid them out in a gently undulating pattern that drifted into the hills to the northwest, where they lost themselves in loops or winding canyon roads. Here oil barons and movie stars would soon build their mansions.

There was no attempt to regulate the demography or architectural esthetics of Beverly Hills. But at coastal Palos Verdes Estates, about twenty-five miles southwest of downtown Los Angeles, an art jury chaired in the early days by Myron Hunt imposed strict rules. This select group reviewed all applications pertaining to the construction of buildings and other changes in the physical environment. Its members expressed a preference for the Mediterranean style in new buildings—meaning red-tile roofs and white stucco. And although there was some concern at the time about the few imposing their taste on the many, the result was a project with

Advertisement for Palos Verdes, *Los Angeles Sunday Times*, April 6, 1924.

remarkable organic unity. By now some of the most stringent jury rules have been relaxed, but the original idea of architectural supervision endures. Unfortunately, another review board, the so-called Homes Association, advocated a different kind of homogeneity for Palos Verdes Estates. Ostensibly to uphold the stability of the community, it levied taxes for the common good, yet it also barred racial and religious minorities from buying homes in the community.

The history of Palos Verdes Estates illustrates the difficulties inherent in the process of planning a community. Obviously a plan is better than no plan at all. But who should do the planning? How is intolerance of minorities

to be avoided without sacrificing social coher-
ence? How are new architectural ideas introduced when some of the involved parties
prefer the status quo? Probably there are no
irrefutable answers to these questions, but it
is at least clear from the handful of examples
of planning discussed here that Los Angeles
and environs are not entirely the result of
random growth. As architectural historian

Reyner Banham wrote in *Los Angeles: The
Architecture of Four Ecologies* (1971), "Planning
in any normal sense is not too common in
Los Angeles . . . though there is more than
might be expected."

These images of Rodeo Drive (above) and Cañon Drive (right) illustrate the undulating plan developed just below Sunset Boulevard in Beverly Hills.

ECLECTICISM IN
DOMESTIC ARCHITECTURE

THE WORD *STYLE* HAS LOST ITS LUSTER in certain circles, perhaps because it suggests something added on, superficial, and therefore unnecessary. But that is what makes it appropriate for the architecture of the 1920s, which was mostly about styles. Although these styles were based on historic precedent, they were not necessarily historically authentic. Instead, they represented an attempt to find something in history's grab bag to delight the eye. Furthermore, these disparate styles rarely competed with one another. All of them might be enjoyed, one playing off its difference from the others. Moreover, a talented architect could create Tudor, Spanish, Islamic, and Anglo-Colonial buildings according to a client's whims. This disregard for strict ideology meant that most domestic architecture in the 1920s was pure entertainment.

Some styles were, of course, favored over others. For example, the architecture of choice for most houses in the 1920s was then called "Mediterranean," a kind of amalgam of principally Spanish motifs with details borrowed from Italy, France, and even North Africa. Its popularity was based not so much on its relevance to California history as it was to the similarity of the

Golden State's climate and flora to that of southern Europe. Oleander, roses, bougainvillea, and cactus thrive in California as they do in the Mediterranean lands, and both regions even share the same kind of sunlight, especially in the afternoon.

In the first decade of the twentieth century these similarities had contributed to the popularity of the style called Mission Revival. But it had drawn upon the myth of an idyllic early California propagated by Helen Hunt Jackson's popular 1884 novel *Ramona*, in which Franciscan missionaries and California

Indians had supposedly lived harmoniously before the Hispanic society was tainted by Yankee avarice and guile. Domestic architecture featured white stucco walls, red-tile roofs with mission-style gables, and Spanish arches. Houses and even railroad stations and hotels were cast in this image and often topped with bell towers. The results provoked some contemporary criticism of the practice of imposing religious details on secular buildings. Critics also noted that many Mission Revival structures were simply awkward.

When Frank Miller, proprietor of the Mission Inn (begun in 1902; additions through 1944) in Riverside, California, saw Myron Hunt's neighboring First Congregational Church (1913), with its beautifully articulated version of Spanish Churrigueresque ornament being built, he commissioned Hunt to design an addition to the inn. What resulted was very different from the original building designed by Arthur B. Benton in 1902. Hunt's work was a fantastic display of baroque forms, which was meant to boost Miller's business. It acted as an advertisement, an unabashed appeal to the vacationer's desire to escape from the humdrum city.

Hunt's ventures into Spanish baroque attracted scant attention compared to the enthusiasm of the multitudes who viewed the Churrigueresque (and Plateresque) forms displayed at the Panama-California Exposition of 1915 in San Diego. The fair's

supervising architect was New York City designer Bertram G. Goodhue, who in the 1890s had twice visited Mexico, the second time in 1899 with his friend, architectural historian Sylvester Baxter. In 1901 Baxter published his monumental ten-volume *Spanish Colonial Architecture in Mexico*, a study with which Goodhue was well acquainted. Although Goodhue usually favored Gothic forms, he chose the more florid Spanish Renaissance and baroque forms for the San Diego exposition. His only fully realized architecture there was the towering California Building (today the San Diego Museum of Man), adorned with ecclesiastical raiment that later was widely imitated; Albert C. Martin's St. Vincent de Paul Roman Catholic Church (1923–25), near downtown Los Angeles, is one vivid example. But the influence of Goodhue's romantic Spanish architecture on his colleagues at the fair caused a sensation in California architecture of the 1920s, not just in churches but in other public buildings.

With a nod to the title of Baxter's book, Goodhue dubbed this public architecture "Spanish Colonial," referring to his observations in Mexico. But the real source of this style was, of course, Spain itself, which Goodhue had also visited. In fact, just before the United States entered World War I, several young American architects, inspired by the San Diego fair, explored the Iberian peninsula and sometimes North

Africa in order to absorb details of its architecture that they might adapt for their own work. They photographed and made drawings of numerous picturesque buildings, mainly in southern Spain.

One of these travelers, Austin Whittlesey, the son of Charles Whittlesey, who had designed many Mission Revival hotels and depots for the Santa Fe Railroad, visited Spain in 1917 and captured its architecture in photographs, in drawings, and eventually in watercolors. He included several of his pictures in a book he titled *The Minor Ecclesiastical, Domestic, and Garden Architecture of Southern Spain* (1917). Its preface was written by Goodhue, who later hired Whittlesey to be a delineator

of interior and exterior renderings for his Nebraska State Capitol (1919–32) in Lincoln. In 1920 Whittlesey published *The Renaissance Architecture of Central and Northern Spain* as a companion piece to the earlier volume. With their illustrations of Spanish farmhouses and images of highly decorated public buildings alike, both books became valuable sources

■ FACING: St. Vincent de Paul Roman Catholic Church (1925), Los Angeles; Albert C. Martin, architect. Clearly this is based on the California Building. ABOVE: California Building (1915), Panama-California Exposition, San Diego; Bertram G. Goodhue, architect. A revival of the highly ornamented baroque of Spain and Mexico.

for the Spanish Revival of the 1920s when a great many books on Spanish architecture were published. Architects noted in these books the dramatic effect of white stucco walls and asymmetrical volumes to which limited but colorful ornament, Spanish or other, might be added. Colored tiles evocative of Islamic architecture were employed, as were potted plants set around a courtyard with a fountain in its center, thus creating a romantic old-world ambience.

Whittlesey's books and many others like them—for example, Arthur and Mildred Stapley Byne's *Spanish Gardens and Patios* (1924)—were readily available to Southern California's architects, who would copy illustrated details and then combine them in new arrangements. Harold Bissner Sr., a Spanish Revival architect in Los Angeles, once told an interviewer, "Put all your details together, and pretty soon you have a nice house" (Polyzoides, Sherwood, and Tice, *Courtyard Housing in Los Angeles*, 1982).

The Mediterranean style that emerged in domestic architecture came more from Spain than from colonial Mexico. Its success encouraged adventures into other historic modes. The result made Los Angeles residential neighborhoods distinctively vibrant. For instance, a Tudor country house with a display of black-and-white work in its gables might stand next to a neoclassical villa. A French Provincial farmhouse would contrast with a nearby cottage that resembled a forest dwelling in Grimm's

■ LEFT: Movie set—*The Mark of Zorro* (1920), featuring Douglas Fairbanks acting against Spanish-style architecture. Notice the exciting display of irregularity in the set.
ABOVE: *Farm House near Cordoba* (1917), a highly picturesque display of asymmetrical forms.

■ ABOVE: Sowden House (1926), Hollywood; Lloyd Wright, architect. Brendan Gill, *New Yorker* staff writer, described this house as "a kind of pre-*Jaws* Jaws." FACING: Spadena House, "Hansel and Gretel House" (1921), Beverly Hills; Henry Oliver, architect. Originally designed as a movie set and office for Irvin V. Willst Productions in Culver City.

Fairy Tales. Lining a street such as Lombardy, which connects Pasadena with the town of San Marino, was a bewildering array of architectural images, many of which resembled stage sets more than private homes. This parade of styles represented what cultural historian William McClung calls an "atemporal historicism, one generally accepted and enjoyed by a public eager to possess the past on convenient terms," in his *Landscapes of Desire* (2000).

Surely one of the strangest of these period revivals was the Mayan, which Frank Lloyd Wright (1867–1959) introduced to the Los Angeles area. Wright claimed in his autobiography that his Barnsdall House ("Hollyhock House") (1917–20) in Hollywood was a real "California Romanza" compared with the "pseudo-romantic in terms of neo-Spanish, lingering along as quasi-Italian, stale with Renaissance, dying or dead of English half-timber and Colonial" so prevalent in the area. Wright did not mention his debt to the Mayan ruins of Chichén Itzá and Palenque, but it is obvious. His slightly later houses in Pasadena and Hollywood were constructed of decorated concrete blocks and reflect an Islamic influence, but they bear traces of the Mayan style as well.

Hints of the Mayan also appear in the local domestic architecture of his son Lloyd Wright (1890–1972), especially in the Sowden House (1926), of which architectural historians David Gebhard and Harriet von Bretton wrote in their *L. A. in the Thirties* (1975), "the central interior court with its pairs of Mayan-like stele, rows of piers and pyramid entrances are what one might expect to encounter in a Hollywood science fiction film of the '30s."

Frank Lloyd Wright was always fascinated by the possibilities of concrete. Just after the Barnsdall House was completed, he began an experiment using concrete blocks strengthened by interwoven steel bars, calling it "tensile-block construction." His description in his autobiography of the attempt was typically florid:

■ FACING: Freeman House (1924), front entrance, Hollywood; Frank Lloyd Wright, architect. This was one of Wright's houses in which he used "tensile-block construction," concrete blocks held together with steel bars. BELOW LEFT: Freeman House, block detail. LEFT: Barnsdall House, "Hollyhock House" (1917–20), Hollywood; Frank Lloyd Wright, architect. A Mayan design of conventional construction.

We would take that despised outcast of the building industry—the concrete block—out from underfoot in the gutter—find a hitherto unsuspected soul in it—make it live as a thing of beauty—textured like the trees. Yes, the building would be made of concrete blocks, but as a kind of tree itself standing there at home among the other trees in its own native land. All we would have to do would be to educate the concrete blocks, refine them and knit all together with steel in the joints and so construct the joints that they could be poured full of concrete by any boy after they were set up by common labor and steel-strand laid in the interior joints.

■ ABOVE: Lloyd Wright House (1928): exterior
wall detail, Hollywood; Lloyd Wright, architect.
RIGHT: Lloyd Wright House, exterior northwest
corner. A late Mayan palace set under an
oak tree.

Wright's first local concrete block house was in Pasadena. Designed in 1923 for Alice Millard and known as "La Miniatura," it did not use tensile-block construction. But his next three did—the Storer, Ennis, and Freeman houses (all in Hollywood and dating to 1923–24). Unfortunately, this method did not prevent these structures from being subject to water and earthquake damage, as was the conventionally built Barnsdall House. Surely he knew that concrete is porous and that rain would eventually cause it to crumble. Needless to say, nature has not been kind to these houses.

As he did for his earlier houses—for example, the Barnsdall residence—Wright would have liked to design the furniture and curtains in all these concrete-block structures. However, Alice Millard, a rare books dealer, insisted on furnishing La Miniatura with her own antiques. Apparently Wright approved, because he acknowledged that Millard's furnishings helped give the interiors "an Old World atmosphere."

The Wrights, father and son, were among the few architects who continued the Arts and Crafts tradition of creating the furniture and hangings for the interiors of the houses they designed. This was a considerable challenge during their Mayan phase since little was known of Mayan furniture. Yet on occasion, the Wrights were equal to the task. Most other residential architects in the 1920s focused on designing houses, leaving the furnishing to their clients, who might hire an interior designer if they had the means. These arbiters of taste became almost a necessity to upper-class and upper-middle-class homeowners, assisting an upwardly mobile segment of the population uncertain of what constituted "good taste." Interior decorators (Wright called them "interior desecrators") usually sought to harmonize the furnishings with the style of the house. They preferred authentic antiques but would settle for new, ready-made pieces when the real thing was not available or when it was too expensive.

E. J. Cheesewright (1880–1957) was the foremost designer of residential interiors in Southern California during the 1920s. Born in England and trained at Gillows in London, he immigrated to New York City in 1905. After stints there and in St. Louis and Kansas City, he moved to the Los Angeles area and in 1918 opened a shop in Pasadena. Determined to serve the wealthy and socially prominent, Cheesewright soon joined several of the

■ FACING: Millard House, "La Miniatura" (1923), the living room of Alice Millard's home, as furnished by the owner, Pasadena; Frank Lloyd Wright, architect. ABOVE: Millard House, "La Miniatura," exterior view.

area's most prestigious clubs—the Newport Yacht Club, the Pasadena Athletic Club, Pasadena's Valley Hunt Club, and the Flintridge Country Club, where he cultivated friendships with future clients. These associations led to commissions to design not only the interiors of city and rural residences but also interiors of hotels, country clubs, and even yachts.

Cheesewright's studios on Pasadena's Green Street were designed by Pasadena architect Louis du Puget Millar, who also planned Cheesewright's home, a pseudo-Cotswold cottage. His offices and sales building complex were done in a modified Georgian mode that was more suggestive of New Orleans than of Virginia; forty-two rooms on two floors occupied its thirty-five-thousand square feet of space. Each salesman had an office on the ground floor, where there were also eight salesrooms, every one decorated in a different, mostly eighteenth-century style. Goods were sent out and delivered to rooms at the rear where there were also workshops. More workspace was on the second floor.

One entered the building through a garden court, off which was a superb "long gallery," or waiting room, furnished in antiques and reproductions made by the Cheesewright firm. Straight ahead was a reception hall with a curved stairwell, whose walls were covered with scenic paper "made in Alsace by a Frenchman [presenting] famous scenes of early American history and of the natural beauties of this country." Around this central space were clustered the period revival showrooms. By the time the prospective clients entered the garden court just beyond the reception area, they must have already been sold on the designer's capabilities.

Cheesewright not only exposed his affluent clients to his own exquisite taste, but he also sold them furnishings and accessories that would suggest they shared it with him. Naturally he dealt in antiques, but when they were not available, his workmen reproduced them or built reasonably accurate facsimiles. When necessary, they even fabricated appropriate ironwork. An article in the May 1925 issue of *California Life* described Cheesewright's successful method, which depended upon establishing high standards of taste and then working collaboratively with each client to achieve a personalized décor. "By special diplomacy each interior is a subtle interpretation of its owner's best qualities," the writer purred, "planned to give the most agreeable complement to his individuality."

Such a happy correspondence between the interior of a house and the character of its client was probably the intent of Cheesewright's interiors for "Greystone," the fifty-five-room Tudor mansion in Beverly Hills designed by Pasadena architect Gordon B. Kaufman for Edward L.

■ Doheny House, "Greystone" (1928): living room, Beverly Hills; Gordon B. Kaufmann, architect; E. J. Cheesewright, interior designer.

Doheny Jr. and built in 1928. The younger Doheny was implicated, with his father, in the Harding administration's Teapot Dome scandal and was the victim of a still-unsolved murder a year after the house was finished. Without betraying the sordid life of its original owner, Greystone still stands, minus its original furniture, and is the site of numerous public and private functions. As designed by Cheesewright, the living and dining rooms reflect the notion that the interior of a house should conform to its exterior style. The heavily beamed ceiling in the living room, therefore, is emphatically Tudor. Most of the furniture also recalled sixteenth-century England. But some of the pieces, such as the couches, were not true to that period, and the powder room oddly evokes the Regency Moderne phase of Art Deco.

The domestic architecture and décor created for the upper classes in the Los Angeles of the 1920s were determined by the catholic tastes of architects and interior designers. Rarely did well-heeled clients balk at the pretense and cost involved. Thorstein Veblen, that acute Midwest-bred observer of the follies of the rich of an earlier era, would surely have called their unquestioning attitude toward domestic design "conspicuous consumption." Some clients, grateful for the counsel of their architects and decorators, would even invite them to their parties and show them off. These latter-day Medici were in awe of artists.

Walter P. Temple Sr. was a member of one of the first Yankee families to settle in the Los Angeles area. He made his money in oil and real estate, and decided to celebrate by building this house on the grounds of his grandfather's ranch. At first he commissioned the well-known Los Angeles firm of Walker and Eisen to build a Mission Revival house, but he fired the firm because he was unhappy with the plainness of the house. To complete the job, he hired the more flamboyant Roy Seldon Price, who had just finished a house in Beverly Hills for movie director William Ince.

Price had just recently moved to Los Angeles from St. Louis, but he quickly noticed the Angelenos' affinity for the Hispanic image. In fact, in the front door of La Casa Nueva, he extended the Iberian Mediterranean style still further by designing it in a version of the Portuguese Manueline style. No one seems to know who crafted the art-glass windows seen throughout the house, but they are certainly colorful. It may be added that it is rather surprising to find this elaborately decorated house and its lovely surroundings in an area of Los Angeles County that is now covered with warehouses that look as if they had been designed by computers.

TEMPLE HOUSE, LA CASA NUEVA
(1919—1923, 1927) CITY OF INDUSTRY

WALKER AND EISEN, ARCHITECTS
ROY SELDON PRICE, ARCHITECT

HOUSING FOR
THE MASSES

TOO OFTEN IN THE HISTORY OF ARCHITECTURE there has been only limited interest in creating esthetically appealing housing for people in the lower-middle-income stratum. In early-twentieth-century America, however, it was discovered that these citizens, all but forgotten amid the general surge of progress, constituted a potential market for designers and contractors. Like people with greater means, the masses of Americans desired stylish single-family homes, preferably with gardens. Thus was born the ubiquitous bungalow, the one- or one-and-a-half-story cottage that by the 1920s was being built singly or in tracts, particularly in urban areas such as Los Angeles.

The basic bungalow design emerged from eighteenth- and nineteenth-century British colonialism. One acquisition of the empire was Bengal, a province of India and the source of the word "bungalow," which was derived from the Hindi *bangala* or the Urdu *bangla* (as in present-day Bangladesh). The native dwelling of that region, a one-story dwelling, was adapted to the style of the colonial administrators by adding sheltered front porches (*varandas*) and the amenities of bedrooms and kitchens.

■ PAGE 83: Aladdin Bungalow—"The Pasadena," breakfast nook (see page 86). ABOVE LEFT: A bungalow in Sri Lanka; the British used bungalows as retreats from the city. ABOVE RIGHT: A 1920s bungalow in Long Beach, with concrete columns made in the shape of tree trunks. Long Beach has preserved its bungalow neighborhoods better than the city of Los Angeles has.

These were built in compounds outside cities throughout the empire and also were constructed as summer homes in the Himalayas and other rural areas. Because bungalows had a bucolic association, they soon became popular throughout Great Britain, where they were built as cottages in the Lake District, as coastal resort communities, and even as workers' houses, as seen in Paisley, Scotland.

In 1880 an American newspaper contained the first mention of a bungalow—on Cape Cod! As a symbol of the resort ideal, this distinctive residential style was seen as a reaction to the complexity of urban life that was troubling to Americans at the time. Not surprisingly, bungalows soon caught on in California, considered in the early twentieth century to be a place of retreat from the headlong pace of progress—a kind of resort. As early as 1905, they were recognized as adjuncts to the Arts and Crafts movement—simple woodsy dwellings that fit into their natural surroundings.

By the 1920s bungalow construction in California was booming. The type was favored by the growing working class—those who could pay their mortgage fees, at least until the Great Depression of the 1930s. Architecturally, these houses lacked the rustic

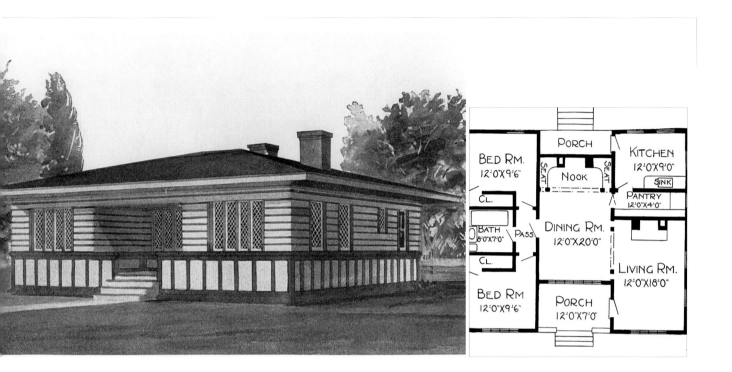

Floor plan labels:

PORCH

BED RM.
12'0"X9'6"

CL.

BATH
8'0"X7'0"

CL.

BED RM
12'0"X9'6"

NOOK

SEAT   SEAT

DINING RM.
12'0"X20'0"

PASS

PORCH
12'0"X7'0"

KITCHEN
12'0"X9'0"

SINK

PANTRY
12'0"X4'0"

LIVING RM.
12'0"X18'0"

■ Radford Bungalow (1908): exterior and floor plan, Catalog 5031. A small California bungalow with style, in this case Prairie style, dedicated to saving space. Notice that there is no entrance hall, only a small hall between the bedrooms to access the bathroom.

character and quality of workmanship that were hallmarks of the earlier pre–World War I bungalows. Their styles ranged from modified Arts and Crafts to watered-down versions of the many period revivals favored by the elite. Their appeal depended, to some extent, on their evocation of rural tranquility. They could be built on the outskirts of cities, thanks to streetcars and automobiles, on lots large enough (barely) for small gardens. After a hard day's work, the owners of bungalows could repair to their cozy homes—quiet refuges from the busy world.

This happy situation in and around Los Angeles was somewhat tempered by the population explosion. As land costs soared, developers accommodated the demand for single-family residences by limiting their

size and at the same time building them on smaller plots of land. These adjustments gave rise to the bungalow court. Ironically, however, the first such concentration of smaller bungalows appears to have been St. Francis Court in Pasadena, which was built in 1909 for affluent vacationers escaping harsh winters in the Midwest and East. Sylvanus B. Marston (1883–1946), a local architect who had opened his office only the year before, designed this eleven-building ensemble in the Arts and Crafts style.

ALADDIN BUNGALOWS

MANUFACTURED BY THE ALADDIN COMPANY
BAY CITY, MICHIGAN

ILLUSTRATIONS BY ALADDIN COMPANY

PAGE 86–87: Exterior with sunroom, artist's drawing, floor plans.

LEFT: Living room.

BELOW: Back bedroom with piano.

The interiors came furnished with pieces from Gustav Stickley's United Crafts and with oriental and American Indian rugs. There were even rooms for servants!

Marston's idea, perhaps suggested by the grouping of cottages in tuberculosis sanitariums or of cabins in mountain camps, was picked up by savvy developers, who adapted it for people of more modest means. The bungalows in Pasadena's Los Robles Court and Bowen Court, both designed in 1910 by brothers Arthur S. Heineman (1878–1972) and Alfred Heineman (1882–1974), were greater in number, smaller in size, and much less lavishly appointed than in Marston's project. They were also placed closer together; this density was a sign of quickly changing times and rising property values. Interestingly, the success of bungalow courts built in various styles during the 1920s spurred the development of motor courts— or *mo-tels*, a term the Heinemans coined after designing San Luis Obispo's Milestone Mo-Tel (1924–25), which still stands.

Although medium-rise apartment buildings began appearing in Los Angeles during the 1920s, residents preferred more space than these structures afforded. If it was necessary to put more people on less land, why not preserve some of the amenities of the recent past? For instance, would it be possible to design Spanish Revival–style structures that would offer a compromise between the privacy of a single-family house and the density of a large apartment building? The affirmative answer to that question took the form of the garden-court apartment complex, which first appeared mainly in West Hollywood and Pasadena.

Generally speaking, these complexes were two-story buildings containing four or six apartments that shared common walls. In the central open area of each building were one or more courtyards with fountains, and, often, luxuriant tropical plants in small private garden spaces. For an added touch of privacy, few of the windows faced the street; instead, they were concentrated on the courtyard side to provide attractive views. The names of some garden-court apartment houses in West Hollywood—Andalusia, Patio del Moro, Villa d'Este—allude to their stylistic provenance in the countries surrounding the Mediterranean. Another, the Roman Gardens (1926), which was designed by brothers Pierpont Davis (1884–1953) and Walter S. Davis (1887–1973), suggests the houses of ancient Rome—despite the fact that the building's tower evokes Moorish Spain or North Africa. The eclectic and talented, albeit amateur, husband-and-wife team of Arthur B. and Nina W. Zwebell provided their garden-court apartment buildings with romantic facades and period interiors; some had two-story living rooms. Nina also ran a small furniture factory that

produced convincing reproductions.

In their book *Courtyard Housing in Los Angeles* (1992), Stephanos Polyzoides, Roger Sherwood, and James Tice call the garden-court apartment buildings "quintessentially Angeleno," expressions of "the ephemeral flamboyance of Hollywood and the imagery of life as some kind of transitional stage set." They represent "the ideal of entertainment in two important ways: defining an interior garden space reflecting the possibility of a life outdoors . . . and developing the exterior courtyard surfaces of court buildings so as to give a dramatic effect." Because they

■ Bowen Court (1913), Pasadena; Arthur S. Heineman, architect; Alfred Heineman, associate. A very early bungalow court for people with modest means.

were usually only two stories tall, they resembled the typical American home; at the same time, they contained multiple units with the kind of pleasing grace notes (noted above) that were not commonly found in apartment houses. Sequestered from the surrounding city, they assured individual privacy while affording some social contact.

Few garden-court apartment buildings were constructed compared with the multitude of bungalows; in Los Angeles alone, there were thousands of these single-family dwellings, often laid out in tracts. Their very proliferation made bungalows seem common and generally lacking in esthetic appeal. In time, they were even ridiculed as being beneath the dignity of architecture—and the very word "bungalow" became derisive.

Without really intending to be experimental the architects and developers in the twenties pioneered the idea that architecture should reach the American middle classes. The building of courtyard apartments tapered off before the Great Depression of the 1930s, but they marked (and still do) a pleasant way to live in an era in which land values were going up so that economies were needed. They preserved the idea of the single-family house without retaining the form. The bungalow that had its brightest day in the twenties was, of course, the ideal solution for the problem of preserving family values in a

changing society, but by the end of the that decade they also became less popular due to rising costs. The prosperity of the period did not reach many people with modest incomes. In fact, most bungalow owners carried mortgages with very high interest rates and became victims of the Great Depression.

Woodrow Wilson, smarting from the attacks on the Versailles Treaty, referred to its opponents—including Henry Cabot Lodge, a Harvard graduate; Wilson was Princeton—as "bungalow-minded," presum-

ably referring to their intelligence quotient. For some, "bungalow" had become a derisive term even before the twenties began. After World War II, the bungalow lived on in the form of tract housing, ranch houses, and Cape Cod cottages, but architecture returned to its association with "the rich, the few, and the well-born."

THE 1920'S ARCHITECTURE OF

GARDEN APARTMENTS

THE ANDALUSIA, EL PASADERO,
PATIO DEL MORO & VILLA SEVILLA

GARDENS

DURING THE SEVENTEENTH AND EIGHTEENTH centuries, English landscape architects and gentlemen amateurs developed elaborate theories about landscape gardening. One of their ideals was the informal English garden, which followed the rules of nature and, at the same time, improved upon them. Andrew Jackson Downing (1815–1852) was America's counterpart to Capability Brown (1716–1783), the iconoclastic English designer of country estates. During a career cut short by his early death, Downing became the nation's leading writer on cottages, country houses, and gardens. Promoting the ideal of cultured domesticity, Downing urged his readers to follow the precedent of informal English gardens in the Romantic tradition, typified by winding paths that led to a Grecian temple or to a Gothic summer house.

Downing was at heart a nurseryman rather than a strict theoretician. He thus struck a chord with his American audience, which was more interested in plants—especially exotic ones—than in theories. What would grow in the new land? George Washington laid out the garden in front of his house at Mount Vernon in a semiformal plan that was shaped, some say, like his wife Martha's guitar. Down by the Potomac River was his experimental

■ PAGE 99: Stourhead Park (1744–65), Stourhead, England; Henry Flitcroft, landscape design; Lancelot (Capability) Brown, Henry Hoare, grounds design. A landmark in the English landscape garden tradition. ABOVE: The original A. N. McNally Estate, Altadena; Frederick L. Roehrig, architect. The typical Victorian garden was not subtle.

his diaries that Washington took delight in trying to grow foreign species.

Farfetched as it may seem, George Washington's interest in cultivating exotica is related to the history of the California garden. If Virginia was an unlikely place to try to grow unusual plants, California—especially Southern California—had an ideal climate for such experimentation. Although the common assumption is that anything will grow in Los Angeles if it has enough water and fertilizer, this is not strictly true. Fuchsia, for example, grows beautifully in Santa Monica, where ocean breezes provide moist air. But it fails to thrive in the semi-desert of Pasadena, even when heavily watered. Local microclimates just a mile or so from one another determine the health of many plants.

Certain species not native to the Los Angeles area nevertheless thrive in its sunlight and fertilized soil. Consider, for example, the ubiquitous palm tree, which— except for a variety of date palms native to the Palm Springs area—was originally unknown in Southern California but is now a symbol of the region. Equally representative of what is botanically possible in California is the eucalyptus, a native of Australia that is now everywhere evident in Los Angeles and environs. Indeed, a school of plein-air painters was named after it.

Even before the 1920s, a determination to cultivate exotic plants and trees in the Los Angeles area led to the development of

garden, where he grew rare plants and trees from seeds that visitors brought him from as far away as Asia. Many seeds failed to come up or even to germinate, but it is clear from

LEFT: Palm trees in Southern California, a non-native tree that is now a symbol of the region.
MIDDLE: *Eucalyptus at Sunset* (1909), a painting by Hanson Puthuff (a Eucalyptus School painter).
RIGHT/FACING: Doheny House, "Greystone" (1928), fountain, with Italian cypress lining the
walk to the pool, Beverly Hills; Gordon B. Kaufmann, architect; Paul Thiene, landscape architect.

ambitious botanical gardens. In 1905, under
the direction of his head gardener, William
Hertrich, Henry E. Huntington began
growing rare species on the grounds of his
vast San Marino estate, which also became
the home of his extraordinary collection
of paintings, rare books, and manuscripts.
He assembled a grove of pepper trees, to
which he was especially attracted, and then
a variety of citrus trees. Later his gardeners
added palm trees, some mature, that they

Hansel and Gretel (above)
Red Riding Hood (below)

The Fox Family (above)
Princess Snowwhite and Her Seven Dwarfs.

transplanted from other collections in California and abroad.

Huntington disliked cactus, but Hertrich convinced him that a collection of these succulents from the nearby desert and from South America and Africa would be a desirable addition; it became one of the greatest cactus gardens in the world. Eventually, extensive plantings of avocado groves, cycads, camellias, rhododendron, and tree ferns were added.

Within the 180-acre garden, straight paths led from one display to another. In 1912 Huntington added a Japanese tea garden: an authentic teahouse, stone lanterns, and other ornaments surrounding an artificial pond. Today another garden extends from the north carriage entrance to the Huntington mansion to an antique fountain and then to a vista of the San Gabriel Mountains in the distance. Originally, only palms lined the grand avenue. They now shade rows of sculptures that remind one of

the garden on the main axis of Versailles. Many changes have been made to the garden since Huntington's death in 1927, when they were opened to the public. For example, some paths were made more sinuous in keeping with English garden theory. And in recent years, a Zen garden designed by Robert Watson was added. A Chinese garden will soon be installed.

Not far from San Marino, on his estate overlooking Pasadena's Arroyo Seco, beer tycoon Adolphus Busch worked with his Scottish gardener, Robert Gordon Fraser, to develop a smaller garden with winding paths. If Huntington's gardens were for the botanist, Busch's thirty-acre landscape was designed for the pleasure seeker. Along with exotic plants, the gardens included pools, fountains, waterfalls, and trails. They also contained surprises, such as small sculptural groups depicting fairy-tale characters: Little Red Riding Hood, Snow White, Little Bo-Peep, and the Three Bears. Like Huntington, Busch had a summer house, but this was reputedly designed to be a facsimile of the Old Mill of Banbury Cross.

The Busch Gardens were opened to the public in 1909. One could reach the site by

HUNTINGTON BOTANICAL GARDENS
(1905–2006) SAN MARINO

WILLIAM HERTRICH, LANDSCAPE ARCHITECT

■ Harold Lloyd Estate, "Greenacres" (1929), Beverly Hills; Sumner
Spaulding, architect; A. E. Hanson, landscape design.

taking the streetcar on California Street (now
Boulevard) to the end of the line at Arroyo
Drive (now Boulevard) and then transferring
to a private car or simply walking south along
Arroyo Drive to the gardens, a quarter of a
mile away. Unlike Huntington's gardens,

which continue to draw enormous crowds,
Busch's extravaganza began to be subdivided
in 1927. By the post–World War II years,
nearly all traces of it had disappeared, though
the Mill of Banbury Cross remains along with
some of the fairy-tale sculptures.

Very few of the many gardens illustrated
in Winifred Starr Dobyns's book *California
Gardens* (1931) still exist. Her photographs

are the chief remains of the marvelous creations of the landscape architects Charles Gibbs Adams, Katherine Bashford, A. E. Hanson, Edward Huntsman-Trout, Paul Thiene, and the partnership of Lucile Council and Florence Yoch. Their landscapes fell victim to luxuriant growth, subdivision, or neglect. In Beverly Hills, silent-screen comedian Harold Lloyd's sixteen-acre estate, with gardens designed by A. E. Hanson, was subdivided; what remains of them is now closed to the public.

Among only a few of these creations that still exist in a condition fairly close to the original are the Virginia Robinson Gardens in Beverly Hills. Mainly dating from the 1920s, they were designed by Charles Gibbs Adams. As Jere Stuart French wrote in *The California Garden and the Landscape Architects Who Shaped It* (1993), Adams "produced hard-edged, geometric gardens of a distinctly Italian Renaissance character, and [was] skilled at hillside design and engineering, using the irregularities of the natural topography to maximum effect." Born in Los Angeles in 1884, Adams studied landscape architecture at the University of California, Berkeley. Leaving Berkeley without graduating, he made the grand tour of European gardens, and, on his return in 1917, opened an office in Pasadena, where he lived in the Garfias Adobe (1841) on the Arroyo Seco. His commissions ranged from the great gardens at the house Bertram G. Goodhue designed for Henry Dater in Montecito

(1915–18) to others at William Randolph Hearst's San Simeon mansion, familiarly known as the Hearst Castle, which he designed under the watchful eye of Julia Morgan, the building's architect.

The Robinson Gardens, situated on a six-acre estate, engaged all of Adams's skills. In the usual European manner, the area near the house (designed in 1911 by Virginia's father, Nathaniel Dryden, in a Beaux-Arts neoclassical style) is formal. A wide mall lined with Italian cypress leads from the house to a pavilion and a guesthouse that William Richards designed in 1924. Mrs. Robinson, widow of the president of Robinson's department stores, held her grand parties on this lawn. She hosted the most famous of these in 1932, inviting the social elite to celebrate her birthday in August on the night of the first full moon. It is said that the flower arrangements and china were selected to match her dress. Behind the guesthouse is the pool where Virginia swam thirty-two laps twice a day until she was eighty-five years old. Beyond this central formal section are brick walks and staircases leading to patios—outdoor living rooms—surrounded by exotic plants and an extensive grove of a variety of palm trees.

The landscape garden has always been a prerogative chiefly of the rich. While some members of the middle class may have aped the affluent in terms of architecture during the 1920s, they lacked the wherewithal to hire landscape designers. As a result, the middle-class garden usually

consisted of a small plot for vegetables; the front yard lawn might be fringed with a floral border of decorative plants such as roses in front of taller shrubs. A banana tree, looking forlorn after a cool winter, might offer some charm for the bungalow dweller, but it was a poor substitute for a grove of palms.

Yet even the rich in Los Angeles were limited in their ability to organize the landscape. The land on which gardens might

■ LEFT: Harvey Mudd House (1920s; house and garden no longer exist); Edward Huntsman-Trout, landscape design; George Stanley, sculpture design. Stanley was also the creator of the Oscar, which is presented at the Motion Picture Academy's annual awards ceremony. CENTER: Landscape plans from *California Gardens* (1914), by Eugene O. Murmann. RIGHT: St. Francis Court (1909; demolished), Pasadena; Sylvanus Marston, architect. FACING: A banana tree graces the front yard of this Santa Monica bungalow, a minimalist version of the Mediterranean style.

grow was cheaper than in the East, but by the 1920s housing was taking up more and more of it. An even greater factor was irrigation. Since Southern California is inherently a dry region with a notoriously unreliable annual rainfall, ever-mounting pressures were being placed on engineered water-supply sources during that decade—as is still the case today. This relative scarcity of both land and water meant smaller gardens, some of which had as their focal point a lone fountain, a sculpture, or a bench. These smaller plots of land dictated classical formality as opposed to the expansive, informal, picturesque garden of the English type with its winding paths and vistas.

VIRGINIA ROBINSON GARDENS
(1920s) BEVERLY HILLS

CHARLES GIBBS ADAMS, LANDSCAPE ARCHITECT

PAGE 114: Pool Pavilion.

PAGE 115: Formal Mall Garden, entry gate.

ABOVE/FACING LEFT: Pool Pavilion, with Rose Garden.

RIGHT: Formal Mall Garden, as seen from the Pool Pavilion.

FACING BELOW LEFT: Pool Pavilion, upstairs card room.

FACING ABOVE RIGHT: Pool Pavilion, back room.

PUBLIC ARCHITECTURE

A MERICAN DOMESTIC ARCHITECTURE REFLECTS our style of life. The home—
the single-family dwelling with a garden—is, in fact, the embodiment of the ideal of the
cohesive family that meets in the evening around the fireplace and talks
about the events of the day—school, office, card club, reading group,
political news, religious issues, ethical beliefs, hobbies, love. On the other
hand, our public buildings represent larger forces outside the domestic
sphere—business, government, schools, theater, concert halls, and social
and religious institutions. Their facades are contrived to make passersby
stop, take notice, perhaps admire—and go in.

It is significant that in a decade in which advertising became a science,
salient public architecture would flourish. It contrasted sharply with the
generally dreary business blocks that were built in the first two decades of
the twentieth century. Critics in those years recognized their dullness. In
the twenties there was a conscious effort to liven up the facades of buildings.
The historical styles became useful in the process of giving them drama.

The steel frame created a rigid pattern on buildings where, according
to the "form follows function" esthetic, the structure of the steel cage was

expressed on the exterior of the buildings in repeated modules. Left without ornament, they were without glamour. As the use of reinforced concrete structures rose in the teens to compete with the steel frame, the problem of monotones regularity was not solved—rhythm without melody. Chicago architect Louis Sullivan had tried to deal with this matter by creating an ornament that in its intricacy contrasted with the prose statement of the steel cage. His venture into decoration was premonitory of what was to come in the 1920s, when thoroughfares such as Spring Street and Broadway in downtown Los Angeles came alive with interpretations of the historic styles. Gothic, baroque, neoclassical, Spanish Revival, and Art Deco—all were thrown together in a wild assortment of images.

Historic precedent lay behind this eclecticism. Sullivan had studied at the École des Beaux-Arts in Paris, where the single, most important principle of design was that the architect should first work out a rational plan and then cover it with the ornament that had been developed over the ages—"plenty to look at" as architectural historian Marcus Whiffen once put it. By the twenties the most important American architectural schools, founded in the late nineteenth century, had based their curriculums on the Beaux-Arts method. It was almost inevitable that in an expansive age the invitation to greater ornamentation would be accepted, as it certainly was in the 1920s.

Once the idea of lavish decoration was accepted, some way had to be found to provide it in large quantities and at a reasonable cost. It lay at hand in the use of terra-cotta, literally "baked earth," a ceramic material, like tile, that had been used by the ancient Greeks and Romans not only for water pipes and cistern heads but also for architectural ornament and sculpture. It had been almost forgotten during the Middle Ages but was reinvented in the Renaissance and employed in various ways in the ensuing years. Then suddenly in the late nineteenth century, there was a huge expansion of the production of terra-cotta for the facing of large buildings. Although many terra-cotta firms developed in California, Gladding, McBean and Company (founded in Lincoln, California, in 1875) was by far the largest producer. In fact almost every important building constructed in the business district of any California city during the 1920s was faced with terra-cotta from Gladding, McBean, which by that time had several factories in the state, including one in the Los Angeles area.

The beauty of terra-cotta, besides its durability, was that in its various glazes it could take on the appearance of stone without being as expensive. For example, the Los Angeles architectural firm of Albert R. Walker and Percy Eisen, when it designed the Fine Arts Building (1925) in downtown Los Angeles, would have liked to use stone but found it too expensive, so the firm faced its building in terra-cotta, which Walker bragged could "out-stone stone." Terra-cotta was admired not only for its versatility but also for its ability to render detail precisely. It could be mass-produced without the errors in execution that bedeviled the human stonecutter's work. Oswald Speir, the manager of the Gladding, McBean operations in Los Angeles, wrote his home office in Lincoln that B. Marcus Priteca, the architect of the Pantages Theater (1920; now the Jewelry Center) in downtown Los Angeles, was pleased with the reproduction of his drawings in the medium of terra-cotta, "but fears that it is a little unrestful in the pose of the figures, a trifle too fine in detail and that the drapery over the figures is too thin and flexible. He does not wish the figures to appear as nudes or to be too suggestive of the contours of the figures."

RIGHT:
Front entrance.

FACING LEFT:
Interior balcony.

FACING RIGHT:
Ground-floor wall.

FINE ARTS BUILDING
(1925) LOS ANGELES

WALKER AND EISEN, ARCHITECTS

Apparently Speir differed drastically with Priteca, for he added, still stressing the capability of terra-cotta to produce fine detail:

I am particularly delighted with the sharp, crisp treatment of the draperies, which, I think, are most intelligently exaggerated to accept the enamel and still carry the proper feeling of the modeling. My only other point would be that Mr. Tognelli [the modeler] find a young woman with real California legs, which would mean a trifle more shapeliness than he has indicated.

Another advantage of terra-cotta for public architecture was its ability to receive color. In 1900 polychrome-glazed terra-cotta was used for the first time in America by McKim, Mead and White in their Madison Square Presbyterian Church in New York. Just before 1920 there was a surge of interest in terra-cotta's ability to enliven architectural detail. The way was paved for the black and gold of the Richfield Building (1929) in downtown Los Angeles and the Security First National Bank (1929) on Wilshire in the Miracle Mile. Thanks to terra-cotta, the Pellesier Building (now the Wiltern) could be blue-green and Andrews Hardware could sport a multicolored frieze.

The Gladding, McBean and Company's Glendale annex, called Tropico Potteries, Inc., produced polychromatic terra-cotta called "Hermosa" for the Pasadena Civic Auditorium, the Los Angeles City Hall, the Biltmore Hotel, and the Mercantile Arcade, all buildings erected in the twenties. Other Gladding, McBean commissions in the period were for the Pacific Mutual Building, Bullocks Wilshire, the Fine Arts Building, the Pellesier Building and the early buildings at UCLA in Westwood.

The materials to produce a colorful display existed. What about the talent to use them wisely and with the best effect? There was no dearth of architects in the 1920s. On the contrary, it is amazing how many well-trained designers had arrived in the immigration of people from the East and Midwest as well as from Europe. The explanation lies, of course, partly in the attraction of the climate, for many architects and/or their spouses had respiratory ailments, but the real pull of Southern California was its prosperity and the possibility of finding lucrative jobs in its growing economy.

The abundance of architects naturally led to competition for commissions and to an attention to projects once they were secured. Personal supervision of work in progress meant good buildings that carried out their promise of fine detail and functional excel-

lence. The scene was dominated by large architectural firms, of which Walker and Eisen was the largest in terms of employees. But a number of other conglomerates, some formed before the twenties, had large practices. Morgan, Walls and Clements was an old firm with a young Stiles Clements as its chief designer. John C. Austin, A. C. Martin, Parkinson and Parkinson, Allison and Allison all had offices in the city. In Pasadena, a center of architectural activity, the firm of Marston, Van Pelt and Maybury was active as was that of Johnson, Kaufman and Coate, whose firm also worked in Beverly Hills. Other smaller architectural offices were sprinkled around the area.

Some of these were important in domestic architecture, but most produced public buildings reflecting the burgeoning economy. It is significant that in spite of the good times, Los Angeles and environs remained an essentially horizontal city. The only building approaching skyscraper status was the Los Angeles City Hall that towered over the urban sprawl until the 1950s, when high-rise arrived as a symbol of even greater economic power.

■ ABOVE LEFT: Security First National Bank (1929), Los Angeles; Morgan, Walls, and Clements, architects. LEFT: Warner Brothers Western Theater (1930–31) / Pellesier Building, now Wiltern Theater, Los Angeles; Morgan, Walls, and Clements, architects; G. Albert Lansburgh, architect; A. B. Heinsbergen Decorating Company, interior design.

■ ABOVE: Grace Nicholson Building (1924), now Pacific-Asia Museum, Pasadena; Marston, Van Pelt, and Maybury, architects. FACING/INSET: El Capitan Theater (1926), now Paramount, foyer, Hollywood; Morgan, Walls, and Clements, architects; G. Albert Lansburgh, theater design.

In the 1920s, as we have seen, the reaction against the boring facades of the steel-frame buildings resulted in more ornament, usually in terra-cotta. Inside, the answer was to expand and enrich the lobbies, some of which were fantastic. This glory in excess was not limited to motion-picture palaces, though it was in this medium that the most spectacular results were achieved. It has been noted that the designers of these theaters often cleverly used mirrors not only to give dramatic depth to their rooms but also to reflect the moviegoers in the midst of finery, thus associating them with the theatrical event—a part of the picture!

The most important designer of the interiors of public buildings in Southern California was Antoon ("Anthony") Bonaventure Heinsbergen (1894–1981), a Dutchman whose expertise in mural and decorative painting got him into interior design. In 1922 he founded the A. B. Heinsbergen Decorating Company and three years later built a studio designed by Claude Beelman, one of the era's most popular architects. Heinsbergen's break came in the early 1920s when Alexander Pantages commissioned him to design the interiors of his national chain of twenty-two theaters. His firm went on to do the interior design of hundreds of other buildings. In Los Angeles he was involved in designing the interiors of the Fine Arts Building, the Los Angeles City Hall, the Elks Club, and the Biltmore Hotel.

MILLENNIUM BILTMORE HOTEL
(1922–23) LOS ANGELES

SCHULTZE & WEAVER, ARCHITECT

In the case of the Biltmore, Heinsbergen seems also to have been associated with Italian painter Giovanni B. Smeraldi (1867–1947), so much so that it is difficult to tell where Heinsbergen left off and Smeraldi began. Possibly Smeraldi, who had worked on the restoration of rooms at the Vatican as a young man, was employed to do some public rooms and Heinsbergen others. Both were painters, and it must be said that both worked in several different styles so that confusion reigns. Nevertheless, Smeraldi's fine hand is seen in his independent work, such as the ceilings of the dining rooms in

Caltech's Athenaeum. He also was responsible for the elegant ceilings of Pasadena's First Trust Building, designed by Bennett and Haskell in 1928. Smeraldi worked on a number of buildings in the Los Angeles area and, in fact, throughout the United States.

The eclectic architects and interior designers of the 1920s created a body of work that was beholden to the past, but they were well trained and exhibited talent; in some cases, such as Wallace Neff in housing and Stiles Clements in public architecture, they showed genius. The money that was at hand certainly helped them. Competition between so many architects of great ability honed the quality of their product. It is true that most of their work was superficial, but it added joy to life. To paraphrase Duke Ellington, "If it looks good, it is good."

■ ABOVE AND FACING: St. Andrew's Roman Catholic Church (1927), Pasadena; Ross Montgomery, architect. ABOVE LEFT: An example of eclecticism in religious architecture, dating back to the medieval period. ABOVE RIGHT: Detail of the front door. FACING: Front entrance portal.

MODERNISM

S O FAR WE HAVE SEEN THE FRIVOLOUS SIDE of the architecture of Los Angeles in the 1920s. But just as the morality of the period had many critics (one of them said that it followed "a single standard and that a low one"), a small group of people in the city proposed an architecture that was the opposite of frivolous, which was, in fact, serious to a fault. These people were what we call the modernists. They would cast aside the period revivals with their "meaningless" ornament and create a new architecture that was stripped to its essentials, which they believed were structure and function. Their watchword was *simplicity*.

This was not the first time Americans had heard the plea for simplicity in architecture. In the eighteenth century, the Shakers sang a hymn that began "'Tis a gift to be simple," and their buildings as well as their furniture reflected that belief. Even earlier, the Puritans had demonstrated it in their meetinghouses, and the Quakers went a step further by excluding any ornament from their religious buildings. Ralph Waldo Emerson, a nineteenth-century Transcendentalist poet and critic, argued that architecture and poetry should be based on elimination of the unnecessary. His

friend, sculptor Horatio Greenough, believed that architects should learn that function was the source of beauty by looking at the economical form of the Yankee clipper ship, though it may be of some significance that when he proposed a monument to James Fenimore Cooper, he envisioned a temple decorated with the classical orders of the Greek Revival.

The most famous American functionalist was Chicago architect Louis Sullivan. A product of the École des Beaux-Arts in Paris, he had accepted its teaching that good architecture began with a good plan, but he was uneasy about the ornamentation of a structure after its function and structure were determined. Ironically he was a great ornamentalist; according to Frank Lloyd Wright, who worked in his office, his genius was in creating ornament and not architecture. But in his essay "Ornament in Architecture" (1892), Sullivan wrote surprisingly, "It would be greatly for our esthetic good if we should refrain entirely from the use of ornament for a period of years in order that our thought might concentrate acutely upon buildings well formed and comely in the nude."

■ PAGE 135: Bullocks Wilshire Department Store: (1928), library clock, Los Angeles; John and Donald Parkinson, architects. FACING LEFT: Old Ship Meetinghouse (1681), Hingham, Massachusetts. This seventeenth-century Puritan meetinghouse, named for the timber truss that frames its roof, is the oldest surviving building for religious worship in the New England colonies. FACING/ABOVE LEFT: Enfield Shaker Village (est. 1793), dormitory, Lake Mascoma, Enfield, New Hampshire. ABOVE: Purdue State Bank (1914), West Lafayette, Indiana; Louis H. Sullivan, architect. LEFT: Purdue State Bank, detail.

■ Miltimore House (1911), South Pasadena; Irving J. Gill, architect.

The influence of Sullivan's ideas on Southern California architecture was especially apparent in buildings designed by Irving J. Gill (1870–1936). After working for Sullivan for two years, Gill moved to California for health reasons. In 1893 he settled in San Diego, where the Mission Revival was already flourishing. Following Sullivan's precepts, Gill adopted the style but eliminated its details. What he created was an architecture of geometric forms and white stucco surfaces that compared well with the work of the European avant-garde.

Gill was almost a prophet without honor in his own country. He had few followers, and

they were insignificant in the modernist cause. The major modernists were in Europe. Walter Gropius, Ludwig Mies van der Rohe, and Le Corbusier preached a machine esthetic that was very similar to Gill's in its results. The machine, its admirers held, was a model of economy, of stripping away the extraneous. Le Corbusier made the point clearly: "A house is a machine for living in." Mies put it even more succinctly: "Less is more." What resulted was an architecture that prized form over expression, geometry over picturesque.

It was not these giants, however, who immediately affected Los Angeles architecture in the 1920s. The new spirit came from Vienna in the late nineteenth century, where a group of painters and architects, contemptuous of the stodgy academic tradition, called themselves Secessionists and dedicated themselves to creating a new art free of the dead hand of the past. By 1900 the architects among them, Otto Wagner and his students Josef Olbrich and Josef Hoffmann, moved away from the expressive wavy line of Art Nouveau into a more spartan style, thus suggesting a modernist inclination.

The Secessionists were moderates, too moderate for Adolf Loos, another Viennese malcontent who deplored the Secessionists' inability to give up ornament. Like Irving Gill, Loos had taken seriously Louis Sullivan's belief that for a time the use of ornament should be set aside. "Ornament is crime," he wrote. It was Loos's radicalism that most strongly affected the Los Angeles scene, because two of his Viennese followers, R. M. Schindler and Richard Neutra, immigrated to the United States and brought his ideas with them. Both became leaders of the modern movement in Southern California. They and their followers made Los Angeles the center of modernism in American domestic architecture.

Schindler arrived first. An admirer of Frank Lloyd Wright, he was drawn to Oak Park just before World War I broke out and was employed by Wright, who in 1919 chose him to superintend the building of Aline Barnsdall's "Hollyhock House" in Hollywood while Wright was in Japan during the erection of the Imperial Hotel in Tokyo. After Barnsdall's house was finished, Schindler opened his own office and began to turn out houses strongly affected by the ideas of Loos and by Wright's romantic manipulation of spaces.

One of the first houses he designed was a duplex (1922) that he built for himself and his wife and for their friends Clyde and Marian Chase on Kings Road in West Hollywood. It was a curious exercise in the way he thought people should accommodate themselves to life in Southern California. Each of the four tenants had their own individual workplace. The house thus had four living rooms joined together, with the women's rooms significantly near the common kitchen (Schindler had no thought of women's liberation). He planned two bathrooms and a guest room but no bedrooms, the sleeping function being

relegated to outdoor "sleeping baskets" on the roof. This somewhat arbitrary solution to the problem of sleep embodied Schindler's fondness for fresh air that was undoubtedly influenced by his erstwhile friendship with Dr. Philip Lovell, whose advocacy of nude sunbathing was well known through his articles in the *Los Angeles Times*. Schindler designed a house for the Lovells on the beach!

The Chases soon moved out of the Kings Road house, but the Schindlers were then joined in 1925 by Richard and Dione Neutra and their child. The Neutras literally moved into the Schindler's small house and stayed for five years. Neutra and Schindler formed a partnership, doomed almost from the beginning by personality conflicts, and eventually Neutra opened his own practice. He secured two important commissions in the twenties—the Jardinette Apartments (1927) and the Lovell Health House (1929)—both of which received immediate recognition for their daring modernism.

Schindler's Lovell House (1927), commissioned as a beach house for the same Dr. Lovell who later chose Neutra to design his city home, was much more dramatic in its use of steel, stucco, and glass than Neutra's more sedate modernism expressed in the same materials. In fact, when Philip Johnson and Henry-Russell Hitchcock were planning their famous "International Style" show at the Museum of Modern Art in 1932, they left out Schindler because they thought

he was too much in the camp of Frank Lloyd Wright, and thus too romantic to be shown alongside the work of the European partisans of the machine esthetic. On the other hand, Johnson and Hitchcock included Neutra's Lovell house and admired its "visible regularity of structure," but it did not stand without criticism. They found its design "complicated by the various projections and the confusing use of metal and stucco spandrels." Neutra's Jardinette Apartments, they said, demonstrated "the first practical application in America of a consistent scheme of design based on modern methods of construction. The ribbon

■ FACING ABOVE: King's Road House, "Schindler and Chase House" (1921–22), Hollywood; R. M. Schindler, architect. FACING LEFT: Wolfe House (1928; demolished), Santa Catalina Island; R. M. Schindler architect. ABOVE: Lovell Health House (1929), Hollywood; Richard J. Neutra, architect. LEFT: Lovell Health House, interior stairway.

windows are splendidly used; but the attempt to make the bands continuous around the facade by painting the occasional intervening wall sections black is a trick of design which is hardly frank."

Hitchcock and Johnson's estimate of the designs of both architects may seem

somewhat quaint, but they do emphasize a salient feature of American modernism. Americans might omit ornament, but by and large, they avoided the severity of the European machine esthetic. Thanks to Wright and other romantic architects who claimed to hate the International Style, the American brand never lost its tendency toward individual expression. Neutra was once heard to say, when his architecture was called International Style, "I am not International Style. I am Neutra!" So much for modernist impersonality!

Architectural historian Eileen Michels has called this humanizing compromise "Soft Modernism." Years later, Henry-Russell Hitchcock admitted that he had been too harsh in his criticism of R. M. Schindler. But Johnson and Hitchcock were certainly correct in noting that Neutra and Schindler had expressionistic tendencies, especially Schindler, whose flair was no doubt strengthened by the style of his paintings, which were admirable contributions to European Expressionism.

Because it was so popular in Los Angeles in the twenties, an even softer modernism of which Johnson and Hitchcock would certainly disapprove was the Art Deco that had first appeared as an antidote to the Art Nouveau. It was given prominence by its use at the Exposition Internationale des Arts Décoratifs et Industrieles Modernes that was held in Paris in 1925, and from which the style took its name. The intention had been to open the exposition in 1914, but World War I intervened. Like the Art Nouveau that it supplanted, it was superficial, with an applied ornament based on zigzag lines with obvious allusions to Gothic architecture. Unlike the International Style, it was easily understood by the general public and was used widely in the United States, particularly in New York City and Los Angeles, but was found on commercial buildings of the late twenties in almost every American city. A kind of people's *moderne*, it appealed to the popular taste for futurism without being the least bit shocking.

BULLOCKS WILSHIRE DEPARTMENT STORE (1928) LOS ANGELES

JOHN AND DONALD PARKINSON, ARCHITECTS

■ FACING: Lobby.

ABOVE LEFT: Window.

LEFT: Tower.

ABOVE: Exterior.

■ Bullocks Wilshire Department Store: Porte cochere mural, *Spirit of Transportation*, by Herman Sachs.

A number of Los Angelenos attended the Paris fair, among them John Bullock, the owner of a high-end department store in downtown Los Angeles. Bullock saw a suggestion of opulence in the Art Deco style that he could employ in opening a new store on Wilshire Boulevard near the heart of an exclusive neighborhood. He commissioned the architectural firm of John Parkinson and Donald Parkinson to design an Art Deco masterpiece that was worthy of the upper middle class to which he would cater. The Parkinsons in turn

commissioned the local designers Feil and Paradise to decorate the interiors while they tried their hands at an impressive exterior. The result, now beautifully converted to a library for the Southwestern School of Law, is one of the great monuments of Art Deco in the United States. Sheathed in terra-cotta with colorful ornament in just the right places and trimmed with copper, today turned green, the exterior was perfectly adapted to attracting discriminating patrons who would arrive in their limousines behind the building and get out under a porte cochere whose ceiling was enriched by a mural, *Spirit of Transportation*, by Herman Sachs.

Entering, the prospective customer, probably intent on having lunch at the fine

restaurant on the fifth floor, would pass a bank of ornate elevators and then go into a great Perfume Hall, lit with tube-shaped Art Deco chandeliers hanging there and in the room to the right. The sportswear department, designed by Jock Peters, featured a large relief sculpture, *The Spirit of Sport* by Gjura Stojano, on one wall (page 134, left). Across the room was a large Art Deco–style clock (page 135). Beyond that was the men's clothing shop, fitted out with cornices and door trim reminiscent of Frank Lloyd Wright's concrete-block ornament on his "La Miniatura" in Pasadena. The upper floors were equally elegant, with frescoes and other intimations of upper-middle-class luxury, but more Louis XVI than Art Deco.

James Oviatt, owner of a men's clothing store that catered to Hollywood stars, had also attended—and been impressed by—the 1925 Exposition Internationale in Paris. The spectacular interiors of his Oviatt Building (1927–28), designed by the firm of Walker and Eisen and located in the heart of the downtown business district, remain in almost pristine condition despite the building having been converted to other uses in recent decades. Oviatt's designers made extensive use of Lalique glass in the storefront, marquee, interior lobby, and salesroom; Oviatt's completely intact penthouse apartment on the thirteenth floor, with its 1920s French furniture and decorative arts, is a classic example of Art Deco style.

FACING: Living room fireplace.

LEFT: Bathroom.

BELOW: Mailbox, elevator door.

OVIATT BUILDING PENTHOUSE
(1927–28) LOS ANGELES

WALKER AND EISEN, ARCHITECTS

■ ABOVE LEFT: Tower.

LEFT: Bedroom accessory, Lalique glass.

ABOVE/FACING: Bedroom.

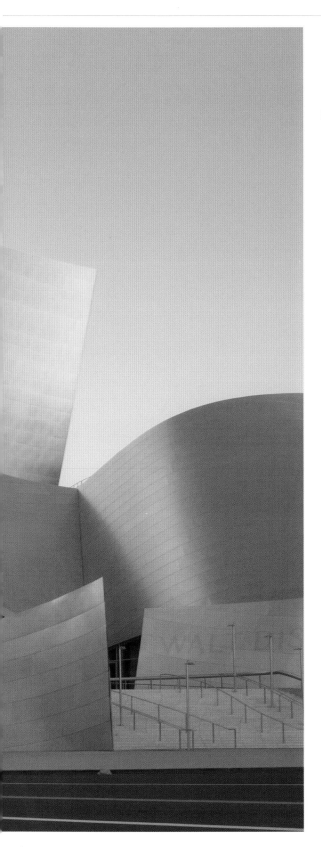

■ Walt Disney Concert Hall (1998–2003), Los Angeles; Frank O. Gehry and Associates, architects. An example of the revival of the "architecture of entertainment."

The golden age of Art Deco lasted only a few years. In the 1930s, Streamline Moderne—or Modernistic, as it was called at the time—became the prevalent futurist style. Its features are evident mostly on theaters, schools, and government buildings. The Great Depression curtailed construction for other purposes. The various types of period-revival architecture likewise suffered from the sick economy; in fact, the Beaux-Arts design basics in which all these styles were rooted—base, shaft, capital—also fell victim to the hard times.

After World War II, domestic architecture took a sober turn, with Cape Cod cottages and tracts of ranch houses becoming popular. In public architecture, the International Style prevailed. Under the direction of Ludwig Mies van der Rohe and his legion of followers, some beautifully articulated buildings—lacking historical precedent and devoid of ornament—were constructed. But for the time being, the "architecture of entertainment" became a thing of the past, only to be revived in a later day.

PHOTOGRAPHIC CREDITS

Image Key:

above (a)	below (b)
left (l)	right (r)
facing (f)	middle (m)
above left (al)	above right (ar)
below left (bl)	below right (br)
facing left (fl)	facing right (fr)
mid-left (ml)	mid-right (mr)

Scattered throughout the text are photographs that I have made during the fifty years that I have lived in Los Angeles County. They are for the record with no claim to artistry. I leave the artwork to my friend and colleague Alexander Vertikoff, whose photographic essays grace this volume and whose single shots also occur in the text.

Occasionally I have used images taken from sources outside the family. Richard Longstreth lent me prints taken from the advertisements of the period. Thanks to Linda Harris Mehr, who heads the Margaret Herrick Library of the Motion Picture Academy Foundation, I was able to get still photographs from several movie sets of the 1920s. Julie Heath representing Warner Brothers Entertainment, Inc., and Richard Gordon of Gordon Films, Inc., also helped in this process.

I am indebted to Carolyn Kozo Cole, Curator of Photographs at the Los Angeles Public Library, for the black-and-white photo of the living room of the Doheny mansion ("Greystone") in Beverly Hills. Ron Fields helped me find it.

Stefanos Polyzoides and Jean-Maurice Moulene provided me with pictures of garden court apartments. Sid Gally found the photo of the living room of "La Miniatura."

Photos by / Photos courtesy of:

Images copyrighted by owners and are courtesy of and/or from the collection of the following:

Alexander Vertikoff, jacket (front, back), 2–3, 5, 6, 7, 8, 10 (l), 24–27, 28 (l, r), 29, 32, 34–35, 37, 39, 40 (m, r), 41, 44, 46, 47, 48, 50–53, 56–57, 58, 59, 61, 68, 69 (bl), 70–71, 72–73, 79–81, 82 (l), 83, 86–89, 98, 102–3, 106–9, 114–17, 118, 119, 122–23, 125, 126, 127, 128–31, 132 (r), 133, 134, 135, 144–45, 146–47, 148–51, 152–53

Burton Holmes, 11, 14 (l)
Elizabeth Moule & Stefanos Polyzoides, 82 (m, r), 94–97
Gordon Films, Inc., 142
Los Angeles Public Library, 77
Margaret Herrick Library of the Motion Picture Academy Foundation, 18 (l)
Occidental College Slide Library, Robert Winter Collection, 40 (l), 49, 69 (al), 110, 138, 140
Pasadena Museum of History (Lian Partlow, archivist), 74
Warner Brothers Entertainment, Inc., 10 (l), 18–19

Images from Books, Brochures, Catalogs, Collections

Page 31: Route of the Pacific Electric Railway, 1923. Based on the map in Reyner Banham, *Los Angeles: The Architecture of Four Ecologies* (1971), 80, which he redrew from an illustration in an old Red Car book. Reproduced here by Rudy Ramos.

Page 65 (r): Farm House near Cordoba (1917), from Austin Whittlesey, *The Minor Ecclesiastical, Domestic, and Garden Architecture of Southern Spain* (New York: Architectural Book Publishing Co., 1917), 48.

Page 74: Millard House, "La Miniatura," from an article by Howell Breece, "Leather and Vellum," *Vo-Mag* 4 (March 1936): 8 [a vocational journal published by the Pasadena Junior College].

Page 87: Aladdin Bungalow, illustration and floor plan by the Aladdin Company.

Page 102 (m): Hanson Puthuff, *Eucalyptus at Sunset* (1909), oil on canvas. From the collection of Robert Winter.

NOTE: all images not credited here are © Robert Winter.

In a book in which the author does not use footnotes, it is especially important that he write a bibliographical essay that reflects the sources of ideas and knowledge from which he drew his material. Thus, since most scholarly works have their own bibliographies, I have tried here to indicate only the books and articles that have most influenced me in my writing, even though I usually have alluded to them in the text. What follows is a personal history of my choicest discoveries that is not intended in any way to be a complete list of pertinent studies.

Introduction

At risk of repetition, I would be remiss if I did not explicitly recognize how valuable Richard Longstreth's *City Center to Regional Mall* (Cambridge, Massachusetts, and London, England: MIT Press, 1997) has been to my writing in this introduction and in several other chapters. Since the "architecture of entertainment," a phrase I borrowed from an article, "Twenties Gothic" (*New Mexico Studies in the Fine Arts*, 7 [1982]) by David Van Zanten, is the subject of our book, I have sampled the growing archive of works on the relationship of 1920s buildings to the silent film industry. I have found Lary May's *Screening Out the Past: The Birth of Mass Culture and the Motion Picture Industry* (New York and Oxford: Oxford University Press, 1980) useful, as I have the collection of essays, *Film Architecture* (Munich, New York: Prestel Publishing, Ltd., 1996), edited by Dietrich Neumann.

The Face of the City

No knowledgeable student of Los Angeles history will fail to observe that I have heavily drawn upon Reyner Banham's brilliant survey of the relationship of transportation systems to the city's growth, *Los Angeles: The Architecture of Four Ecologies* (New York: Harper and Row, Publishers, 1971). Merry Ovnick's *Los Angeles: The End of the Rainbow* (Los Angeles: Balcony Press, 1994) has also been useful. I should also mention the fact that my personal observation has been a strong factor in this chapter.

Planning the "City Beautiful"

Much of the material in this chapter is a condensation of the long essay, mainly researched and written by David Gebhard, in our *Los Angeles: An Architectural Guide*, 4th ed. (Salt Lake City: Gibbs Smith, Publisher, 1994). More on Myron Hunt's Beaux-Arts plans and buildings will be found in my *Myron Hunt at Occidental College* (Los Angeles: Occidental College, 1986). Bertram Goodhue's plan

for Caltech is covered by Romy Wyllie in her *Caltech's Architectural Heritage* (Los Angeles: Balcony Press, 2000). The plan of the Palos Verdes Estates is discussed by Thomas P. Gates in an article, "The Palos Verdes Ranch Project," *Architectonic* 6 (May 1997). A valuable study of the Pasadena Civic Center is Ann Scheid Lund's *Historic Pasadena* (San Antonio: Historical Publishing Network, 1999), Chapter 5.

Eclecticism in Domestic Architecture

William Alexander McClung's *Landscapes of Desire: Anglo Mythologies of Los Angeles* (Berkeley and Los Angeles: University of California Press, 2000) is a bright book that covers a lot of territory but is especially good on the Hispanic image of Los Angeles. The architects of the 1920s period revival architecture have not been well covered in recent scholarship. Alson Clark's *Wallace Neff: Architect of California's Golden Age* (Santa Barbara: Capra Press, 1986) will have to do for that most important period revivalist until several promised studies appear. *Johnson, Kaufmann, Coate: Partners in the California Style* (Santa Barbara: Capra Press, 1992), a catalog edited by Joseph N. Newland, is a good introduction to a successful Pasadena firm. A general overview is David Gebhard's "The Spanish Colonial Revival in Southern California (1895–1930)," *Journal of the Society of Architectural Historians* 25 (May 1967), though his inference that American Modernist architecture is related to the white stucco walls of the Spanish Revival seems far-fetched.

There is no history of the interior design profession in California—or elsewhere. Art Deco seems to have been the style that caught the eye of the historians. My information on the E. J. Cheesewright firm comes largely from the National Register of Historic Places registration form. Frank Lloyd Wright's ideas concerning exterior design are best gathered from his book *An Autobiography* (New York: Duell, Sloan and Pearce, 1943), though they are often confusing. Writings by him and on his work are, of course, plentiful.

Housing for the Masses

The literature on bungalows, whose heyday was in the 1920s, is by now vast. An introduction to it is in my *American Bungalow Style* (New York: Simon and Schuster, 1996). Bungalow courts still need attention, as do motels. Stefanos Polyzoides, Roger Sherwood, and James Tice have recognized the beauty of the garden court apartments of the 1920s in their *Courtyard Housing* in *Los Angeles: A Typographical Analysis* (Berkeley, Los Angeles, London: University of California Press, 1982).

Gardens

In his excellent *California Gardens: Creating a New Eden* (New York, London, Paris: Abbeville Press, 1994), David Streatfield has included a very complete bibliography. In addition to Streatfield's analyses of selected gardens, I have also profited from a reading of Jere Stuart French's *The California Garden and the Landscape Architects Who Shaped It* (Washington, D.C.: Landscape Architecture Foundation, 1993) and Victoria Padilla's *Southern California Gardens: An Illustrated History* (Berkeley and Los Angeles: University of California Press, 1961). No garden book could be more charming than William Hertrich's *The Huntington Botanical Gardens, 1905–1949* (San Marino: The Huntington Library, 1949), which mixes personal asides on the Huntingtons with an account of how their gardens grew.

Fascinating because they were written just after the 1920s when their materials were fresh are Sidney B. Mitchell's *Gardening in California* (New York: Doubleday, 1932) and Winifred Starr Dobyns's *California Gardens* (New York: The Macmillan Company, 1931), both containing photographs of many gardens that no longer exist.

Public Architecture

By the 1920s concrete had taken precedence over steel as the favored building material for public buildings. Construction in concrete came in three methods—(1) poured into wooden frames, (2) steel-reinforced cage construction similar in form to the steel frame, and (3) Frank Lloyd Wright's "tensile-block" construction. A rather surprising book on this subject—surprising because it recognized early in the history of concrete construction the special contribution of Southern California architects to this phenomenon—is *The Ferro-Concrete Style* (New York: The Architectural Book Publishing Co., Inc., 1928) by Francis S. Onderdonk Jr., a professor in the College of Architecture at the University of Michigan. It was reprinted in 1998 by Hennessey and Ingalls. The story of American terra-cotta has been well, if briefly, told by Susan Tunick in her introduction to Gary F. Kurutz's *Architectural Terra Cotta of Gladding, McBean* (Sausalito, California: Windgate Press, 1989), which covers the history of this major terra-cotta firm in California in the 1920s. Indeed, the firm still exists.

There is a great deal of misinformation on the role of Giovanni Smeraldi in the decoration of the interiors of the Biltmore and other 1920s buildings. From what one can gather from Margaret Leslie Davis's usually authoritative *The Los Angeles Biltmore: The Host of the Coast* (Los Angeles: The Regal Biltmore Hotel, 1998), Smeraldi was a ceiling painter. But often he worked with Antoon (Anthony) Bonaventure Heinsbergen, a Dutchman who was just as gifted as Smeraldi in interior design. Presumably Smeraldi worked on ceilings and Heinsbergen on walls.

Modernism

Esther McCoy, who worked for a time for R. M. Schindler, was the first significant critic to recognize the importance of modernism in the architecture of Los Angeles. Her *Richard Neutra* (New York: George Braziller, Inc., 1960) called the attention of architectural critics and historians to the fact that in domestic architecture Los Angeles architects were pioneers in the modernist movement. She wrote on the work of Schindler in a chapter in her *Five California Architects* (New York: Reinhold Book Corporation, 1960). David Gebhard joined the Schindler admirers in his *R. M. Schindler, Architect* (Los Angeles: Los Angeles County Museum of Art, 1967). McCoy added further information on Schindler and Neutra in her *Vienna to Los Angeles: Two Journeys* (Santa Monica: Arts + Architecture Press, 1979). More recent works on the two architects are Thomas S. Hines, *Richard Neutra and the Search for Modern Architecture* (New York, Oxford: Oxford University Press, 1982), and Elizabeth A. T. Smith and Michael Darling, *The Architecture of R. M. Schindler* (Los Angeles: Museum of Contemporary Art in Association with Harry N. Abrams, Publishers, 2001).

The Art Deco phase of modernism has been well covered nationally. Comments on the local scene are Margaret Leslie Davis, *Bullocks Wilshire* (Los Angeles: Balcony Press, 1996) and David Gebhard, *The Richfield Building 1928–1968* (Los Angeles: Atlantic Richfield Company, 1968/1970). Pauline Schindler, then the wife of R. M. Schindler, wrote an extremely insightful article on Bullocks Wilshire shortly after it was completed: "A Significant Contribution to Culture: The Interior of a Great California Store as an Interpretation of Modern Life," *California Arts and Architecture* (January 1930): 23–25.